Harold Barclay

People Without Government

An Anthropology of Anarchy

Preface by Alex Comfort

Kahn & Averill, London
Left Bank Books, Seattle, WA., U.S.

This completely revised edition published in 1990 by
Kahn & Averill
9 Harrington Road, London SW7 3ES

British Library Cataloguing in Publication Data

Barclay, Harold
    People without government : an anthropology of anarchy. –
2nd. completely rev. ed.
    1. Anarchism, history
    I. Title
    335.8309

    ISBN 1-871082-16-1

First published in the United States by
Left Bank Books
4142 Brooklyn NE, Seattle, WA 98105

ISBN 0-939306-09-3 (US)

Printed and bound in Great Britain by
Halstan & Co. Ltd., Amersham, Bucks

Contents

Preface

Anarchism is that political philosophy which advocates the maximization of individual responsibility and the reduction of concentrated power – regal, dictatorial, parliamentary: the institutions which go loosely by the name of "government" – to a vanishing minimum. It has no connection with bomb-throwing radicals: it has, in fact, been a point of view which has attracted biologists, such as Kropotkin, the founder of ecology, and anthropologists. To advocate it one must practise considerable self-abnegation, because the type of community it envisages cannot, for obvious reasons, be prescribed. One cannot say with Colonel Blimp "Dammit, if the blighters won't be democratic we must make 'em". It is the blighters themselves who have to choose.

In this book Harold Barclay gives a scholarly account of a number of societies which do not accept the idea of Authority as natural – in fact, it does not occur to them. The documentation is fascinating, and it has its uses as an answer to the mythologies of "primitive man"which have propped up conventional political theories from the XVII century on.

The question which must occur to most readers, however, is one of relevance – rightly, in view of the contemporary excesses of "sociobiology" and the currency of theories based on white rats and Trobriand Islanders. Pygmies and Eskimos neither organise railroads nor operate social services: modern emulators like Makhno and Durruti, or the kids who organise free communes, look quixotic. The serious man's problem with the anarchist wish to be rid of government is not, I think, that he quarrels with the idea that governments today represent little beside psychopathology, or that politics as we practise it is the art of preventing the

possible. His doubts arise from the complexity of society, which
looks irreversible, and the need for forward planning: in fact,
the charge-sheet of many modern governments is concerned not
only with the abuses they commit, but with their culpable failure
to plan. In the past, the excesses of power were offset by its ability
to provide coordination one put up with the psychopathology of
King Henry VIII because a strong king was manifestly preferable
to multiple local war lords. But with the growth of a technologically
sophisticated public it has become plainer and plainer that today
teleonomic, or purposive, planning has become almost wholly
divorced from government. It is conducted by experts, while
authority devotes itself to play-therapy. Some scientists, who find
warnings ignored and resources squandered on pyramids, Maginot
Lines and Five Year Plans unrelated to reality, talk about the day
when computers will do the planning. Unfortunately, if they did,
the playtherapy group would programme them.

Faced with this, the "serious man" withdraws into anti-politicism,
or, in America, populism (which substitutes free enterprise and the
Devil take the hindmost for the anarchist recipes of mutual aid
and direct action). He would be quite willing to learn from the
Inuit and Pygmies if one could convince him that their forms of
organisation had any lessons one could apply to a modern, complex
community.

I think they have. The challenge "go run a modern state like a
pygmy village and see what happens" misses the rather unusual
cast of mind which anarchists seek to impart. Unlike Marxism
or democratic capitalism, which are institutionalised theories,
the rejection of authority as a social tool is an attitude, not
a programme. Once adopted it patterns the kind of solutions
which we are disposed to accept. Nor in order to be an
anarchist does one need to wait until society shares the same
attitude. Anarchists do not plan revolutions but when they
become numerous, and the type of thinking which underlies the
social organisation of the small groups Harold Barclay describes
becomes common, the thinkers constitute active, unbiddable and
exemplary lumps in the general porridge of society. If numerous
enough, they begin to affect the types of choices which societies
make. Mutual aid begins to constitute a serious alternative to
administrative services, general dissatisfaction begins to turn to
civil disobedience. If "revolution" occurs in consequence it is in
the form of an assault by alarmed authority, loath to see its
kingdom fail, on the increasingly ungovernable public, in other
words counterrevolution. The growing awareness is threatened
by inertia, by cooption, and by the set non-Pygmy habit of mind

which comes from centuries in which our political muscles have atrophied.

Nor, in order to influence the course of society, do anarchist-minded thinkers have to be wholly successful any more than the Chartists were successful. The Chartists did not secure a single demand of the Charter, but they reformed the parliamentary process. The surviving government of a state whose citizens thought and acted anarchistically would be an Irish democracy – one where the head of authority is held under water whenever it steps out of line. Poland, at the time of writing, may be headed in that direction. And indeed not only anarchist thinking, but even anarchist techniques, such as unanimity instead of a majority vote, are getting incorporated into such places as unions and protest movements which a few years ago would have used parliamentary procedure as a matter of course.

My own view is that anarchism is an attitude, not a programme: that attitude has enzymatic effects on the society in which it is widespread leading quite possibly to an adhocracy, an illogical compromise between Simon Pure anarchism and some of the old apparatus, rather as republican sentiment has been transmuted into a constitutionalism which illogically retains a monarch as a kind of blocking piece, to restrict the excesses of elected representatives. There are probably instances where decision-making has to be concentrated, provided the hot breath of the public is on the neck of the decision-maker. One would not now agree with the protoanarchist Godwin that it is a betrayal of liberty to play in an orchestra if it has a conductor. Where Barclay's anthropological accounts are important is not as blueprints for complex societies, but as expositions of the attitudes of humans who have found no need of Authority. Faced with other environments, these attitudes will lead to new social structures, since man is an adaptive thinker, but as attitudes they are not time or place-determined. We are likely in our time to see many local and neighbourhood exercises whose form is classically anarchist, plus a growing tide of protest, some principled, some merely exasperated, in which anarchist modes of action and thought may be embodied. A society in which protest is fully effective has no need of a set revolution, and such a society, whether triggered by Marxist stupidity and dogmatism or Friworld military psychopathology, is an attainable goal. Studies such as these have accordingly more than academic importance.

Alex Comfort

Introduction

Anarchy is most often equated with chaos or seen as some crackpot scheme advanced only by bomb-throwing, wild-eyed maniacs. Certainly it is an idea which has not been taken seriously by most. Although in recent years there has been a slight increase in appreciation of anarchist theory, to the extent that a greater number now consider it worthy of mention in serious discussion, it remains largely ignored. The anthropologically demonstrated fact that anarchy is possible is frequently overlooked.

Over the past several generations, anthropologists, through their ethnographic research, have documented innumerable stateless and governmentless societies throughout the world and throughout time. And even the devotees of Marx point to these as indicators of some earlier stateless stage of human cultural evolution. Nevertheless there is some considerable reluctance to define these societies as anarchies. Even amongst anthropologists there are those so imbued with their own cultural traditions that they will go to any lengths to avoid recognising these systems for what they are. Because they believe social order can exist only where there is government and law, they stretch the meanings of these terms to cover what is clearly not government at all. In an anthropology textbook, Hammond has written[1]: "Even when the population is large, relatively dense, and somewhat diversified, the absence of government does not necessarily imply the presence of anarchy" (239). Hoebel, who later changed his mind, has so defined law and the state, and so interpreted the data of numerous cultures, as

---

[1]See Bibliography for this and subsequent references.

to make every society a state with law (1958, 467ff). And earlier, both Clark Wissler and George Murdock included a 'government' as a 'universal' of culture (Wissler, 1923; Murdock, 1945).

Other anthropologists readily recognise the widespread existence of stateless societies, some even call them 'functioning anarchies'. They see the need to demonstrate the existence of such societies as a task long since accomplished and believe we should move on to more important problems. However, it has been my experience in more than 30 years of teaching anthropology that, among students, about the most firmly held myth is the one that no society can exist without government — and its corollary that every society must have a head. If modern day students have given up the religion of the church, they have not budged from the religion of nationalism and statism. It is the latter which affords the source of unity — the cementing element — in contempoary 'pluralistic' society. Thus, the myth of the necessity of the state and of government is decisive for that unity, as decisive as belief in God was for the unity of Medieval society. In the universities, political 'science' departments are the chief centres for the promulgation of this myth.

One task of this book, then, is to present examples of anarchy. Thereby we will demonstrate that there are human societies which fit the criteria of anarchy and should be recognised for what they are.

There are also other reasons for this book. I will be suggesting that anarchy is by no means unusual; that it is a perfectly common form of polity or political organisation. Not only is it common, but it is probably the oldest type of polity and one which has characterised most of human history.

In the course of this presentation, attention will be given to the kinds of social, economic, technological and ecological contexts which appear to be conducive to anarchic systems. We must consider the oft-made proposition that if anarchies or governmentless, stateless societies exist, they could do so only in the most simple form of human culture and in the smallest type of grouping.

An important aim of this book is to give some idea of what anarchy in practice is like. In this we must consider the various ways in which order is maintained within anarchy. This in turn is related to the more general problem of the dynamic interplay between freedom and authority which characterises human society. In connection with this we must observe how anarchy can, and does on occasion, appear to degenerate into despotism, a process which also entails a consideration of the origins of the state. In general, then, we will try to address the question: is there anything to be learned from these anarchic polities?

Perhaps, finally, this essay will provide a critique of anarchist theory and contribute, therefore, to an improved understanding of the problems of freedom in society.

There are similarities between what is proposed for this investigation and some of the works of Kropotkin, namely, his *The State: Its Historic Role* and *Mutual Aid*. These works were a factor in my decision to enter the field of anthropology and also stimulated my writing of this book. I would like to think that this book adds to, and improves upon, Kropotkin's pioneering investigations in this subject.

I

On the Nature of Anarchy

On anarchy and anarchism

Our first task must be to clarify the meaning of anarchy in relation to a variety of different terms. Let us begin by considering anarchy and anarchism. These must be distinguished from one another, just as one distinguishes 'primitive communism' from Marxian communism. The latter is an elaborate sociological system, a philosophy of history and an idea for a future condition of society in which property is held in common. 'Primitive communism' refers to a type of economy, presumably found among 'archaic' or 'primitive' peoples, in which property is held in common. By property is to be understood the crucial resources and means of production of wealth. In fact, what is communally held in such societies is invariably land; tools, livestock, and many other kinds of resources (eg, fishing sites) are individually owned. In any case, Marxist theory does not identify primitive communism with the intended Marxist communism. One might say that implicitly it is held that the historical process involves a grand cycle where humans commence with primitive communism and ultimately return to communism at a higher level — which is somewhat reminiscent of the progressive-cyclic theory of Giambattista Vico.

As we distinguish between the two communisms, so we must also distinguish between anarchy and anarchism. Anarchy is the condition of society in which there is no ruler; government is absent. It is also most clearly associated with those societies which have been called 'archaic' and 'primitive', among other pejorative adjectives. Anarchism is the social political theory, developed in 19th century Europe, which incorporates the idea of anarchy, but does so as part of, and as a result of, a broader, self-conscious theory of values which makes human freedom and individuality paramount. Thus, in anarchist theory, the first premise is something which Josiah Warren called the sovereignty of the individual and from this it follows that government and state are oppressive of individual freedom and should be abolished. But, at the same time, the anarchist looks to the abolition of other institutions similarly interpreted as oppressive: the Church, the patriarchal family and any system which appears to enshrine 'irrational' authority. Anarchist theory is egalitarian and anti-hierarchical, as well as being decentralist. Discrimination based on 'race, colour, or creed' or sex are always anathema. Anarchists were probably the first advocates of women's liberation.

In place of the old system, anarchist theory advocates self regulation and voluntary co-operation. Social relations are to be carried out through free contractual agreements of mutual or equal benefit to all parties involved. For Proudhon 'mutualism' was a basic cornerstone of anarchy. His mutualist conception has an interesting similarity and concordance with the contemporary anthropological theory of Mauss and Levi-Strauss, since mutualism may be readily seen as reciprocity. To Levi-Strauss, reciprocity as a mutual exchange is the fundamental structural principle of society; it is a kind of 'category of thought', so fundamental as to be imbedded in the human mind. Pierre Clastres, following in the tradition of Levi-Strauss, argues that 'coercive power', that is, both state and government, are unreciprocal since a ruler receives more than a subject, so upsetting the balance of equity. Therefore, state and government are in opposition to the basic principles of social life: society is against the state. In the final chapter I shall return to Clastres' thesis and the general subject of reciprocity and the emergence of coercive power. Here I only wish to indicate that anarchist theory and anthropological theory do impinge upon one another.

In addition to mutualism, Proudhon and Bakunin, among others, also stressed the idea of federalism, designed to facilitate relations between increasingly larger and more widespread groups of people. The initial building blocks of the federalist plan are the local, 'face to face' groups, either of neighbours or persons with common occupational interests — in any case they have a common mutual interest in working with each other for one or more ends. Such groups form and concern themselves with achieving their specified goals. In order to facilitate these ends they 'federate' with other similar groups to form a regional federation and in turn regional federations join with others to form yet a broader federation. In each case the power invested in the organised group decreases as one ascends the different levels of integration. As

Bakunin and others said, the system was to be 'built from the bottom up and not from the top down'. Each member of a federation has a right to withdraw if in disagreement with the majority's proposed action.

It is interesting to note here the similarity between anarchist federalism and the segmentary lineage system characteristic of many anarchic polities, especially in Africa. In both cases the sum is composed of segments and each segment of sub segments and so on. In both cases the most effective authority is in the smallest unit, decreasing directly as one ascends to broader levels of integration, so that at the 'top', the ultimate federation has little influence whatsoever. In both cases, as well, we have a technique for establishing a broad network which draws innumerable small groups into a large integrated whole. One major contrast between the two systems, however, is that federalism is based upon the co-operation between groups — the principle of mutualism or reciprocity — while for segmentary lineages the operative principle is opposition or conflict between groups of the same level.

Anarchist federalism should not be confused with the kind of 'confederacy' advocated by such men as John Calhoun and other early 19th century American political thinkers. Anarchists would be sympathetic to such a view only in that it proposes to strip central government of most of its authority, permitting member states to withdraw from the system if they see fit. However, from an anarchist point of view, Calhoun and his sympathisers were inconsistent, in that they were primarily concerned about maximizing the power of the several states within the Union. Had they been interested in the freedom of the individual unit members, they would also have recognised the legitimate right of the counties to withdraw from states, of towns to withdraw from counties and of individuals to withdraw from towns.[1]

Anarchism is in sum a complex theoretical orientation. It should not, however, be seen in any sense as a single monolithic conception, or a grand theoretical system to be compared, say, with Marxism. Anarchism, on the contrary, entails several related, but often distinct, points of view. And no anarchist theoretician has ever presented an integrated theoretical system. Yet all anarchist theory shares a common concern for the individual and freedom, opposition to the state and a desire to establish a system of

---

[1]Proudhon's latterday ideas on federalism have recently been raised in connection with the discussion of the nature of Canadian federalism and thus of the Canadian nation (cf. Proudhon, 1979).

voluntary co-operation. It is obvious that the sort of society envisioned by anarchists does not exist and, except for a few isolated and short lived attempts, has never existed. Nevertheless, we do have numerous examples of anarchy — societies without government and without the state.

Just as Marxist communists might not be thoroughly pleased with a functioning 'primitive communism', so we cannot expect anarchists to approve extant anarchic polities. It is obvious that many would be horrified by some of their characteristics. While these societies lack government, as we shall see, patriarchy often prevails; a kind of gerontocracy or domination by the old men is not uncommon; religious sanctions are rampant; children are invariably in a 'second class' position; women are rarely treated in any way equal to men. Indeed, there are invariably strong pressures to conform to group traditions. But since they are highly decentralised, lacking government and the state, they do exemplify anarchy. And thus we must look at such systems as examples of the application of anarchy.

It may be argued that to employ the term 'anarchy' for a major group of human societies is ethnocentric and confuses ideology with social classification. It is to take a highly emotionally charged word, one with a very clear ideological connotation, identified with Euro-American cultural traditions, and to apply it cross-culturally when those in the other cultures would clearly lack the ideology and values of the anarchist. Thus, not only is the word distorted, but so also is the meaning of those cultures.

But if this is true of the word 'anarchy', it applies equally to the use of such words as 'democratic', 'government', 'law', 'capitalist', 'communist' and a host of others employed daily by social scientists, yet derived from ordinary speech. Social science is full of terms in common usage which are applied to social contexts in other cultures. There are certainly dangers to such a procedure. It is easy to carry extraneous ideological baggage along with the term. On the other hand, if we cannot at all make such cross-cultural transfers, we are left with a proliferation of neologisms which become pure jargonese, enhancing obfuscation rather than clarification. There are, after all, *types* of social phenomena which occur throughout the world. Scientific understanding is not furthered by a kind of radical phenomenology which makes every cultural item, every individual perception, unique. I believe many anthropologists, in their own projection of personal and cultural values, have obstinately refused to apply the one truly clarifying term to those numerous societies which are without government and are, therefore, anarchies.

Social order and authority

One of the universal characteristics of mankind, or of any species for that matter, is that it survives and thrives in the context of ·some kind of order. That is, humans have peace of mind where behaviour and events are on the whole predictable. We are animals of habit or animals of custom – traditionalists. Behaviour in human societies is, therefore, stanardised and deviations are punished. A society by definition has order and structure and operates with regularised, relatively fixed modes of behaviour. The term 'society' implies that the compenent members are operating according to some 'rules of the game'. Such rules can be extremely vague and open to conflicting interpretations, or they may be very specific and explicit. In any case, there are guidelines without which we would be lost in a sea of *anomie*. Part of the problem of the modern world is that many of these guildelines have become so ambiguous that the level of general anxiety of the population increases. It is clear that where there is no structure, there is no order and there is no society. And, as the first lesson in any anthropology or sociology course points out, humans without society are not human. But another part of that first lesson is that there is an immense amount of variation within human society, including the amount and kind of structure and order.

Having said this, let me add that humankind often seeks a holiday from routine and structure. Max Gluckman pointed to what he called 'rituals of rebellion', which are periods in which the populace is expected to behave — within limits — in a manner counter to normal expectation. Thus there is the 'Mardi Gras', which is a traditional relaxing of behaviour before the commencement of the exacting observations of the Lenten season. We have Hallowe'en as a traditional time when children are permitted a short expression of rebellion against the adult community.

Victor Turner has suggested that there are two countercurrents in a society: one of structure and the other of *communitas* or anti-structure. The latter expresses the spontaneous, the unplanned and the ecstatic, as a kind of reaction to the usual, predictable and structured. This in a way parallels Proudhon's view that authority and liberty operate as antinomies within any society, each acting so as to delimit the other. In terms of these polarities, anarchism as a social theory is allied with communitas and liberty. Like Thoreau, anarchists are critical of those elements within a culture which become so engrained as to be stultifying and superficial or empty rituals. They look with favour on the new and the untried. Perhaps Nietzsche's call to live dangerously has some relevance here.

On occasion, the anarchist sympathy for communitas has appeared to go to extremes. Thus Hippies, in their rejection of modern structures, sometimes reject every form of structure so as to enshrine dirt — the ultimate of disorder. But while, of all social theories, anarchism has more sympathy for communitas, it is still not opposed to structure, to order or to society. Indeed, Proudhon once wrote that liberty is the mother of order not the daughter. The issue for anarchists is not whether there should be structure or order, but what kind there should be and what its sources ought to be. The individual or group which has sufficient liberty to be self-regulating will have the highest degree of order; the imposition of order from above and outside induces resentment and rebellion where it does not encourage childlike dependence and impotence, and so becomes a force for disorder.

The relation of anarchy to power, authority, politics and political organisation is another misunderstood area. In human groups some manoeuvring for power characterises the relationship between individual members. The intensity and emphasis on the contest varies from one culture to another and from one individual to another. The cultural values of the Pygmies to be discussed and also of such Pueblo Indian groups as the Zuni and Hopi, play down attempts by individuals to stand in the forefront, although one cannot say that the desire to influence others is absent. And within every culture there is variation. Some people strive more than others; a few even opt out. Nevertheless, the contest for power manifests itself in some fashion within each human group.

Power means the ability to get others to do what you want them to do. Thus, someone who convinces ten others to follow orders has more power than someone who is able to get only one to obey. But this depends on all other things being equal, since, for example, someone who controls the one individual who knows how to use a nuclear detonating device can have more power than someone who controls the behaviour of a million ordinary men and women.

Power means influence — convincing others by logical argument, by the prestige of one's status or rank, by money or bribe. Or it means implied or overt threat of injury — either by physical or psychological means — and the ability to carry it out.

The contest for power is an important dynamic force in the social group — a major mechanism by which the group undergoes change over time. The 'push and pull' of members not only causes 'palace revolutions', that is, shifts in the personnel of the less powerful and the more powerful, but leads as well to changes in rules and values.

Ralf Dahrendorf, a German sociologist who is certainly no

anarchist, presents a thesis in a way amenable to anarchist thought, particularly as an answer to Marx. Dahrendorf suggests that the conflict for power is central in a society; Marx was primarily concerned with one feature of the power complex, namely, economic power. This emphasis has meant that those who follow Marx devalue the non-economic dimensions of power. Consequently, we find the world full of peoples' democracies in which the oppression of ordinary people is no less than it was before the 'revolution'. Marxism in practice has tended to transfer the forces of power from the capitalist to the professional bureaucrat and military officer, primarily because it does not see that the central problem is the problem of power itself. The anarchist insists upon addressing this larger issue.

Neither anarchy nor anarchist theory deny power; on the contrary, in anarchist theory this is a central issue for all human societies and the limiting of power is a constant concern. Bakunin recognised the great human drive for power (Maximoff, 248ff). Anarchy is, after all, the condition in which there is the maximum diffusion of power, so that ideally it is equally distributed — in contrast to other political theories, such as Marxism, in which power is transferred from one social group (class) to another. It is, of course, true that much anarchist thinking regarding power has been muddled by 'utopian' dreaming of the ideal society where no-one infringes on anyone else. Godwin and Kropotkin, for example, believed that in the course of time the human race would evolve towards a condition where all were good to their fellows and did not try to take advantage. But other anarchists are not such optimists about human nature; if they were they would not be so worried about the uses and abuses of power.

Max Weber stressed the difference between power and authority. In any society, individual members recognise certain others as having authority within specified realms. Thus, in modern society, members accept as *legitimate* the right of certain individuals to carry and, where 'necessary', to employ firearms, in order to apprehend suspected law breakers. These policemen invariably wear special dress. Members of this society do not recognise as legitimate the use of force by others, such as gangsters. In both cases coercive force is employed. In the first the power is authority since it is seen as legitimate and right; but the second is not authority; it is the illegitimate use of power. Something of this kind of distinction can be identified in all societies. Yet a significant modification of Weber's terminology is in order. Most Canadians would eagerly subscribe to the notion that the power of the Ottawa government is legitimate, but some would only acquiesce to that power. The several generations of colonial rule of the Dutch in Indonesia, for example, commenced as a pure case of the imposition of brute and raw force. But with the passage of time it acquired a certain 'legitimation', so that the power became authority in Weber's terms. But it becomes legitimate power because the Indonesians learned to acquiesce: they grew accustomed to the situation and tacitly accepted it. Raymond Firth has noted that power acquires some kind of support from the governed either because of "routine apathy, inability to conceive of an alternative or acceptance of certain values regarded as unconditional" (123). Most authority commences as the raw power of the gangster and evolves into the 'legitimate' authority of tacit acquiescence. This is certainly the history of the nation state. Fried observes that legitimacy is the means by which ideology is blended with power. The function of legitimacy is "to explain and justify the existence of concentrated social power wielded by a portion of the community and to offer similar support to specific social orders, that is, specific ways of apportioning and directing the flow of social power" (Fried, 26).

No philosopher or social theorist accepts the legitimacy of 'raw' use of power and none rejects totally and completely any and all kinds of authority. Even the anarchist recognises that there is a place for legitimate authority. An anarchist conception of legitimate authority was long ago intimated by Proudhon: ". . . if man is born a sociable being, the authority of his father over him ceases on the day when his mind being formed and his education finished, he becomes the associate of his father. . ." (n.d.,264). Later Bakunin wrote: "We recognise then, the absolute authority of science. . . Outside of this only legitimate authority, legitimate because it is rational and is in harmony with human liberty, we declare all other authorities false, arbitrary and fatal" (Maximoff, 254).

Paul Goodman in *Drawing the Line* writes of natural coercion in which the infant is dependent upon his mother or the student upon the teacher — cases in which teaching is involved with the intent of increasing the independence of the one to attain the level of the other (1946). I don't know whether Fromm ever read Proudhon, Bakunin or the early Goodman, but certainly his view of the nature of authority closely parallels and further explicates that of his anarchist predecessors. Fromm distinguishes, as does Bakunin, between 'rational' and 'irrational' authority. Rational authority has its source in competence; it requires constant scrutiny and criticism and is always temporary. It is based upon the equality of the authority and the subject "which differ only with respect to the degree of knowledge or skill in a particular field". "The source of irrational authority, on the other hand, is always power over people" — either physical or mental power (9).

Stanley Milgram has said that people appear to believe that those in positions of authority, including politicians, are the most knowledgeable. But perhaps this is only wishful thinking in an attempt to justify their authorities. People delude themselves into thinking that through the electoral process they put those in office who are intellectually superior.

Modern society has many in authority who have earned rationally the right to authority, but it has many whose claim to authority is irrational and they are our politicians, judges and policemen. These the anarchist rejects, accepting only rational authority. Anarchists recognise that there are specialists, that is, authorities in various realms, who are accepted as such because of their expertise. Yet one can readily see the potential danger inherent even here, that those holding one form of authority may seek to extend their power so that rational authority is transformed into irrational authority.

Closely related to the concept of authority is that of leadership. Again, no one can deny that there are individuals who appear in every human group who stand out as influential persons for one reason or another. The anarchist movement has long accepted leaders within its own folds, even though it has remained suspicious of the general idea. Although group leadership is a universal of human social organisation, it is, at the same time, necessary to stress that leadership is conceived differently amongst different peoples. The Pygmies and Hopi of Arizona express an anarchist distrust of leaders, such that each individual seeks to avoid the leadership role, blending into the group as much as possible.

Since societies have order and structure and must deal with the problem of power, they are therefore involved in politics. When we use the word politics, we are concerned with power and its uses in a human group. Not only do all societies have politics, but they have political organisation or political systems — that is, standardised ways of dealing with power problems. Political organisation is not a synonym for government. Government is *one* form of political organisation. Politics may be handled in a variety of ways; government is just one of those ways. Thus it is clear that even anarchism as a theory does not deny or oppose politics or political organisation. It is, on the contrary, very political.

In the broadest sense politics can be applied to any kind of social group. That is, there may even be politics within the family — where clearly the distribution of power between father, mother, son and daughter is a major issue. A local club also has politics in a similar small-scale fashion. Ordinarily, however, when one speaks of politics or political organisation, one does not think of the internal affairs of the family. Political organisation applies more to 'public' affairs — relations which are territorial and cut across kinship groupings. Politics involves a substantial geographical area — a community, or at least an extensive neighbourhood. Yet even this kind of conceptualisation leads to ambiguity as to whether one is dealing with political or family affairs. We may have a confrontation between two groups related by kinship, but beyond the level of extended family (for example, two patrilineages), which would be considered at least as a quasi-public affair. Nevertheless, the terms of address employed and the atmosphere of the exchange will unmistakably be those of kinship.

Social sanctions
Neither anarchy, nor anarchist theory in sum, is opposed to organisation, authority, politics, or political organisation. It is opposed to some forms of these things, especially to law, government and the state, to which terms we must now proceed.

Radcliffe-Brown proposed the term 'sanctions' to apply to the manner in which a social group reacts to the behaviour of any one of its members. Thus, a positive sanction is some form of expression of general approval. A soldier is given a medal; a scholar an honorary degree, or a student an award; mother kisses little junior for his good behaviour, or daddy gives him a piece of candy. A negative sanction is the reaction of the community against the behaviour of a member or members; it expresses disapproval. Thus, a soldier may be court martialled; a scholar fired or put in jail; a student failed in course work or ostracised by fellow students and the child slapped by his parent. It seems obvious that it is the negative sanctions which become most important in any society.

Sanctions may also be categorised as being 'diffuse', 'religious' or 'legal'. Here my interpretation deviates slightly from that of Radcliffe-Brown. Diffuse sanctions are those which are spontaneously applied by any one or more members of the community. Crucial to the conception of diffuse sanctions is the notion that their application is not confined to the holder of a specific social role. They may be imposed by anyone within a given age/sex grade or, occasionally, there may be no limit to who may initiate them. This is the meaning of diffuse: responsibility for and the right to impose the sanction is spread out over the community. Society *as a whole* has the power. There is no special elite which even claims a monopoly on the use of violence as a sanctioning device. Further, when and if sanctions are applied is variable, as is the intensity of the sanctions imposed.

Diffuse sanctions include gossip, name calling, arguing, fist fighting, killing and ostracism. Duelling and formal wrestling matches are less widespread forms. Inuit have ritualised song competitions in which two opponents try to outdo one another in insults before an audience which acts as judge. Diffuse sanctions may be resorted to by an individual or a group. And their effectiveness is enhanced as the entire community joins in participation in the sanctions. Vigilante style action and feuds are common forms of diffuse sanction which depend upon collective action.

In many societies, fines and other punishments are meted out by an assembly. Radcliffe-Brown calls these 'organised' sanctions. Yet they are still not 'legal' but have the character of diffuse sanctions, of a more formalised type, *if* the assembly has no authority to use force in executing its decisions. In such instances the assembly members act as mediators rather than judges and are successful to the extent that they can convince two disputing parties to come to some compromise.

Diffuse sanctions are a universal form of social regulation; if a social group has nothing else it will have various techniques which can readily be classified as diffuse sanctions.

Religious sanctions involve the supernatural. 'Black magic' may be performed against a person; one may be threatened with the eternal torment of hell, or encouraged with a positive religious sanction promising everlasting ecstasy in heaven. The Nuer leopard skin chief may get his will done by threatening to curse another. The Ojibwa Indians believed infractions of the rules led to the acquisition by supernatural means of specific kinds of diseases. Thus, religious sanctions may either have a human executor, as in the case of a curse which must be invoked, or be seen as automatic, as with the Ojibwa belief, or the idea that breaking out of the ten commandments commits one to hell fire. In another respect religious sanctions are either those which are intended to bring forth punishment in this life, or those which are for an after-life: physical versus ultimate spiritual punishment.

Legal sanctions involve all expressions of disapproval or approval of the behaviour of an individual wherein:
a such expressions are specifically delegated to persons holding defined roles, one of the duties of which is the execution of these sanctions;
b these individuals alone have the 'authority' to threaten use of violence and use it in order to carry out their job and;
c punishments meted out in relation to the infraction are defined within certain limits and in relation to the 'crime'.

Policemen, justices of a court, jailers, executioners and lawmakers are examples of those who may enforce legal sanctions. In our society they collectively constitute a government. The state, through its agent the government, declares it has the monopoly on the use of violence against others within society, meaning that only certain agents of the state, for example, policemen, can take a person off the street and put him or her in jail. Only certain collectivities, that is, the courts, can determine guilt and assess a punishment in accord with what others, the lawmakers, have established as law. Finally the punishment connected with a legal sanction is fairly standardised and precise. A person found guilty of robbing a store will receive, say, a year to ten years in prison.

Legal sanctions are laws. Laws exist where one has specific social roles designed, or delegated, to enforce regulations by force of violence, if necessary and where punishment has certain defined limits and is not capricious. Law exists where you have government and the state; conversely, if you have a government you have law. Legal sanctions, and thus law and government, are not universal, but are characteristic of only some human societies — albeit the most complex ones. Such societies also, it should be borne in mind, retain a peripheral position for both diffuse and religious sanctions.

Malinowski suggested that the term 'law' should be applied loosely to cover all social rules which have the support of society (Malinowski, 9-59). Such usage, however, obscures the fundamental and important difference in the means by which different rules are enforced. Law and government are invariably associated with rule by an elite class, while governmentless societies are invariably egalitarian and classless. Hence, Malinowski's loose usage obfuscates the important difference concerning who, or what, enforces regulations.

It should be clear that any society characterised by the prevalence of legal sanctions can hardly be called anarchic. As we shall note in considering some of the case studies below, there are marginal examples. There is no clean-cut line between anarchy and government. The relation of anarchy to diffuse and religious sanctions, however, requires some futher clarification. In the social theory of anarchism the idea of voluntary co-operation has been made the positive side of the coin of which abolition of government is the negative. Where the idea of voluntary co-operation is so critical to anarchist thought, it is important to consider it in relation to the nature of functioning anarchic polities, giving special attention to the employment of diffuse and religious sanctions.

Voluntary co-operation, like its antonym, coercion, is a highly ambiguous term. From one point of view nothing may be seen as purely voluntary and all acts as being in some way coerced. For one thing, it might be said that conscience, ego, id, 'the inner spirit' or what have you, are fully as coercive forces as the policeman, or as public ostracism. However, coercion may be best conceived as a relationship of command and obedience, wherein the commanding force is either human or supernatural, but is always external to the individual person. Ideally, for true voluntary co-operation to prevail, there must be no such forms of external coercion. Yet, in fact, even anarchists themselves accept the use of such coercive force and limit voluntary co-operation. In their everyday activity, in their writings and in their own creation of anarchist communes and societies, anarchists use a variety of diffuse sanctions. Some have advocated and applied what are clearly legal sanctions.

It is sometimes difficult to distinguish the type of society envisioned by a Bakunin or Proudhon from a decentralised federal democracy. Towards the end of his life, Proudhon seems to have moved away from his advocacy of voluntary association, towards a sort of minimal state. ". . . (I)t is scarcely likely", he writes in *Du Principe Federatif*, "however far the human race may progress in civilisation, morality, and wisdom, that all traces of government and authority will vanish" (20). For him anarchy has become an ideal type, an abstraction, which like the similar ideal types, democracy and monarchy, never exist in a pure form, but are mixtures of political systems. "In a free society, the role of the state or government is essentially that of legislating, instituting, creating, beginning, establishing; as little as possible should it be executing. . . . Once a beginning has been made (for some project) the machinery established, the state withdraws leaving the execution of the new task to local authorities and citizens" (45). Proudhon has become an advocate of a federal or confederal system, in which the role of the centre is reduced "to that of general initiation, or providing guarantees and supervising . . . (T)he execution of its orders (are) subject to the approval of the federated governments and their responsible agents" (49). He cites the Swiss confederation with approval. "If I may express myself so", Proudhon had written in a letter of 1864, "anarchy is a form of government or constitution in which the principle of authority, police institutions, restrictive and repressive measures, bureaucracy, taxation, etc, are reduced to their simplest terms" (quoted in Buber, 43). We are left wondering if the elder Proudhon would now not feel more at home with such early American opponents of centralised government as John Taylor of Caroline or John Randolph of Roanoke, even John Calhoun.

Bakunin, who absorbed most of Proudhon's federalist ideas, presents a similar problem. In describing his idea of a federal system in the *Organisation of the International Brotherhood*, Bakunin makes some disconcerting statements: "The communal legislatures, however, will retain the right to deviate from provincial legislation on secondary but never on essential issues. . ." while the provincial parliament "will never interfere with the domestic administration of the communes, it will decide each commune's quota of the provincial and national taxation". There are to be courts and a national parliament as well. This national parliament "will have the task of establishing the *fundamental principles* that are to constitute the *national charter* and will be binding upon all provinces wishing to participate in the national pact". The national parliament "will negotiate alliances, make peace or war, and have the exclusive right to order (always for a predetermined period) the formation of a national army" (Lehning, 72-73). Bakunin's anarchy sounds like a decentralised federalist democracy. Yet a year after writing this document he seems to redeem himself for anarchy in an essay on *Federalisme, Socialisme et Antitheologisme*: "Just because a region has formed part of a State, even by voluntary accession, it by no means follows that it incurs any obligation to remain tied to it forever." "The right of free union and equally free secession comes first and foremost among all political rights" (Lehning, 96).

Kropotkin favourably described the early Medieval city commune as an anarchistic system, when, as we shall note below, it surely had a governmental structure. The same may be said concerning the 'anarchist collectives' established in the Ukraine in 1917 and later in some of those in Spain. Even such an individualist anarchist as Josiah Warren saw the need for organised militias. And most anarchists have legitimised military force to achieve their ends, or have considered it an unfortunate necessity. In a word, anarchists have sometimes been equivocal about legal sanctions, to say the least.

In focussing on highly centralised realms of coercion in modern society such as the state and the church, they have also tended to neglect the sometimes more oppressive force of such diffuse sanctions as gossip and ostracism. Nevertheless, there is an important difference between the coercion of the state and the coercion of diffuse sanctions, which may in part justify anarchist reliance on the latter while rejecting the former. In the state or government there is always a hierarchical and status difference between those who rule and those who are ruled. Even if it is a democracy, where we suppose that those who rule today are not rulers tomorrow, there are nevertheless differences in status.

In a democratic system only a tiny minority will ever have the opportunity to rule and these are invariably drawn from an elite group. Differential status is not inherent in diffuse sanctions. Where a group or individual employs gossip or ostracism against another person, that person may freely use these same techniques. Where differential status is associated with diffuse sanctions, such as in the command position of the father over his son, we do have a form of coercion which begins to approach that of government. Yet still the father role has the quality of a rational authority and a young man may expect eventually to 'graduate' to a position of greater equality with his father, eventually achieving fatherhood himself. In no diffuse sanctions is there a vesting of the power to employ violence into the hands of a restricted group of commanders.

Anarchism as a social theory cannot, and I believe in actuality does not, reject all forms of coercion. While its advocates may wield the slogan of voluntary co-operation, it is recognised that this too has limits. For anarchists there is a tacit and, for many, an overt recognition of the legitimate use of some kind of force in some circumstances and this force is what anthropologists refer to as diffuse sanctions. Indeed, as psychologists have informed us and as Allen Ritter has lately reiterated, these sanctions are imperative for the development of personality. The growth of the individual's self image relies upon knowing what others think of his or her behaviour. At the same time, the operation of sanctions instills awareness of others and so builds community by building empathy (Ritter, 1980).

Concerning religious sanctions, anarchist theoreticians have generally looked upon religion as another oppressive system aimed at curbing the free expression of the individual. Michael Bakunin, especially, saw God and the state as two great interrelated tyrannical ogres which must be destroyed. All well-known anarchists at least opposed the church — religion being seen as an organised and hierarchical social structure. Even Tolstoy agreed in this, although his anarchism derived from his interpretation of a Christianity which stressed the literal acceptance of the teachings of the Sermon on the Mount.

The Catholic Worker Movement is a rather unusual development within American anarchism. Led by a convert to Catholicism, Dorothy Day, it professes both an adherence to the principles of pacifist anarchism and to the Roman Catholic Church — a kind of Catholic Tolstoyan movement. Few outside this movement have understood how anarchism, or for that matter any moderately libertarian doctrine, could be reconciled with Roman Catholicism and its dedication to an absolutist monarchy — the papacy — and to a rigid hierarchical structure.[1]

Most anarchists see any religion as an authoritarian system, but are all religious sanctions necessarily incompatible with anarchy? I think not. We must appreciate the distinction made above between those religious sanctions which require human mediation and those which are 'automatic'. A religious sanction which is least compatible with anarchy and takes on some of the character of a legal sanction, is one which can only be invoked by a specific individual as part of a formal office and where there is consensus that such a person has a legitimate monopoly on the power — ie, the authority — to impose sanctions. The priest is the best example of this. On the other hand, where the power to invoke religious sanctions is available to the many and not legitimately monopolised, we have a situation which parallels diffuse sanctions. A punishment which is believed to come directly from God or some other supernatural force, does not require human intervention and is more on the order of subjugation to natural occurrences such as storm and earthquake. Indeed, it is quite clear that punishment by one's conscience is a sanction of this order. Those religious sanctions which parallel diffuse sanctions, as well as those which require no human intermediary, do not seem incompatible with anarchy as we have here conceived it.

Government and the state

Conceptions of government and the state and the relationship between them are often confused. Marxists and some anarchists, including Bakunin, declare their opposition to the state and desire to replace what is called 'political' government with a government over 'things'. But this seems like playing with words and sloganeering. Any 'things' are going to be manipulated by people and will therefore be seen as in need of governing because people are involved. So it is still a government over people. Further, one cannot abolish the state and still have a government, since the latter is the institutional apparatus by which the state is maintained.

Nadel (1942, 69-70) has given three specific characteristics of the state and in doing so has also indicated the role of government in the state. First, the state is a territorial association.

---

[1]The *Catholic Worker* newspaper allowed the appointment of a priest as Church censor and Dorothy Day herself has said she would stop its publication immediately if so ordered by the Church.

It claims 'sovereignty' over a given place in space and all those residing within that area are subject to, and must submit to, the institution of authority ruling or governing that territory, that is, the government.

While the state is a territorial entity, it is often an inter-tribal and inter-racial structure. The criteria for membership are determined by residence and by birth. Membership is ordinarily ascribed, although one may voluntarily apply to join if one immigrates and settles within the territory of the state.

The state has an apparatus of government and this is to some degree centralised. The government functions to execute existing laws, legislate new ones, maintain 'order', and arbitrate conflicts to the exclusion of other groups or individuals. It comprises specific individuals holding defined social roles or offices. Crucial to the definition of such roles is the claim to a monopoly of the legitimate use of violence within that territory. The part played by the different role holders in using violence may vary so that there can be a highly differentiated system or division of labour (cf the discussion of legal sanctions above). All are in any case part of a single integrated monopolistic institution. Such a situation differs, for example, from the role of the Inuit shaman who may threaten a victim with violence, since the shaman cannot claim a monopoly on its legitimate use.

The ruling group in any state tends to be a specialised and privileged body separated by its formation, status and organisation from the population as a whole. This group collectively monopolises political decision. In some polities it may constitute an entrenched and self-perpetuating class. In other more open systems such as a democracy, there is a greater circulation or regular turnover of membership of the ruling group, so that dynasties or other kinds of closed classes of rulers do not ordinarily occur. This, of course, contributes to the illusion of equality of power in a democracy and obscures the division between rulers and ruled.

Fundamental to both government and the state is the employment of violence to enforce the law. This may be variously viewed as either the imposition of the will of the ruling group, or as a device to maintain order, keep the peace and arbitrate internal conflicts. In fact states and governments fulfil all these functions by enforcing the law. It is theorists of the left and especially anarchists, however, who emphasise that the paramount and ultimate end of all law enforcement is to benefit the ruling interests, even though there may be positive side effects such as keeping the peace. They would further emphasise that the existence of the state is conducive of strife and conflict since as a system based upon the use of violence it thereby legitimises and incites it. The state is further predicated upon the assumption that some should be bosses giving orders while others should be subordinates — a situation which can only irk the subordinates and frustrate them and, thus, become yet another provocation of violence. Democratic systems may ameliorate this situation but they do not cure it. By their nature state and government discourage, if they do not outlaw, the natural voluntary co-operation amongst people, a point made by Benjamin Tucker and more recently in some detail by Taylor. Anarchist theory is therefore clearly opposed to Hobbes' thesis that without government society is nasty and brutish. Indeed, anarchists set Hobbes on his head and argue that the world would be more peaceful and amenable to co-operation if the state were removed. And, clearly, the anthropological record does not support Hobbes in any way. Stateless societies seem less violent and brutish than those with the state.

Above all, the state and government are organisations for war. No more efficient organisation for war has been developed. It is interesting and perhaps ironic that right-wing and anarchist theoreticians have converged in recognising the significance of violence to the life of the state. Machiavelli's practical guide to the operation of a state has disturbed many a naive believer in democracy, since the Italian politician recognises force and fraud as the obvious central mechanisms for the success of any state. Von Treitschke, the German historian whose greatest hero was Frederick the Great, observed that "without war no State could be. All those we know of arose through war and the protection of their members by armed force remains their primary and essential task. War, therefore, will endure to the end of history as long as there is a multiplicity of States . . . the blind worshipper of an eternal peace falls into the error of isolating the state, or dreams of one which is universal, which we have already seen to be at variance with reason" since a state always means one among states and thus opposed to others (38). "(S)ubmission is what the State primarily requires . . . its very essence is the accomplishment of its will" (14). "The State is no Academy of Arts, still less is it a Stock Exchange; it is Power. . ." (242).

The pioneer British anthropologist, Edward B Tylor, wrote in his *Anthropology*, "A constitutional government whether called republic or kingdom, is an arrangement by which the nation governs itself by means of the machinery of a military despotism" (156).

Nietzsche, who contrary to popular opinion was no friend of the state, noted its predatory nature: "The State (is) unmorality organised . . . the will to war, to conquest and revenge. . ." As a predator the state attempts to become larger and larger, ever expanding its sphere of influence and subjugation at the expense of other weaker states. It is true that in the course of time in this interstate struggle most states opt out of the conflict and resign themselves to becoming satellites of larger states, realising they cannot effectively compete. It is also true that the giant states may not always seek to gobble up weaker states, because they find it better for their own interests to keep such states as ostensibly independent entities. Thus, in the modern world, we have super powers which are in the midst of the struggle for expansion, carrying on the traditional predatory role of the state — the United States, Soviet Union, China, France, the United Kingdom (now marginally). There are innumerable satellite states of each of the big predators. There are those — usually known as 'Third-world' states — which may try small order predation against neighbouring states, but on the whole they keep their independent status and opt out of full conflict because they are buffers between, or pawns of, the big predators. Finally there are a few states such as Switzerland and until recently Lebanon which are perpetually neutral zones; the big predators do require such zones in which to operate, particularly for information gathering purposes.

Conclusion
The classification of sanctions discussed above may now be summarised in relation to political systems by means of the following diagram presented as a continuum with anarchy, where there is no government, at one end and archy, where the state and government clearly exist, at the other. Under anarchy only diffuse and certain supernatural sanctions are operative, while archy is characterised by the prevalence of legal sanctions. In the middle, between the two poles, there is a limbo which may be seen as a marginal form of anarchy or a rudimentary form of governmental or archic system. There are many anomalous cases of this kind and we shall consider some of these below. Such entities may possibly be considered as transitional examples from anarchy to statism. As Lowie has said, states do not appear full blown out of the stateless condition; they too must evolve or develop and this takes time.

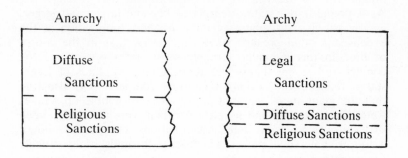

Maine in his *Ancient Law* was the first to explicate an evolutionary typology of tribal or stateless society on the one hand and the state type society on the other. The first was based on kinship ties, in which every member believed he was related to all others in the group. Members obeyed a head man, not as a ruler of a state, but as a senior kinsman, as head of a family, a father. Early societies were all of this type and in the course of time some evolved into societies with a different basis of membership — that of territory. 'Local contiguity' rather than kinship became the basis for deciding the ultimate authority. Such a society entails a government and a state. Gluckman has noted that Maine meant to stress that the 'revolution' in social order comes about when dwelling in a certain territory was sufficient to grant citizenship without having to create some kinship tie either by marriage, adoption, or through inventing a genealogical connection. "The alteration comes when a kinship idiom to express political association is no longer demanded" (86).

My continuum should not be interpreted as an evolutionary scheme, in which culture history is a one-way street where tribal or anarchic societies only become state type societies, while the reverse does not occur. At any point in time, individual societies may be placed along the continuum. In addition, any given society may have different positions in the course of its history. The major thrust of history seems to be the transformation of stateless into state societies, but, as we shall note below, there are examples as well of the reverse and of societies which seem to oscillate back and forth between the two opposite poles. In addition, let us not forget that even if the trend of history and evolution favours the change from anarchy to archy, this does not thereby make that process right and good.

II

Some Observations on Procedure

In selecting the various societies discussed in the following chapters, I have attempted to obtain a wide ranging diversity in terms of geography and cultural type. At the same time an effort has been made to employ a sampling which offers distinct and different solutions to the problem of order in anarchy. In other words, emphasis has been placed on drawing examples of varying kinds of sanctions and styles of leadership. Some cases are included whose anarchic nature will clearly be controversial. They may represent cases of marginal anarchy or marginal 'statism'.

We may distinguish among the several examples of anarchic polities between those which are 'unintentional' and those which are 'intentional'. The latter are deliberate, planned attempts by individuals to initiate a social order according to some preconceived programme. To use another descriptive adjective, they are 'Utopian' experiments along anarchist lines. Most of the sample are 'unintentional', the kind of societies which, like nearly all those in the human adventure, have grown "like Topsy", in the absence of any overall conscious plan.

Finally, concerning these unintentional societies, it should be borne in mind that for most of them the conditions described no longer obtain. With the advent of European imperialism these anarchic polities — which are clearly the least understood by European colonialists of all non-European political arrangements — were transformed to fit into the pattern of government and order as conceived by the masters. In the descriptions which follow, however, the present tense will be used so as to suggest an 'ethnographic present'.

The discussion of the several anarchic polities is placed within the context of a typology of societies long in vogue in anthropological circles: that is, according to their primary mode of subsistence. Thus, some are hunters and gatherers of wild animals and plants; others are chiefly simple gardeners or horticulturalists primarily dependent upon cultivating domesticated plants with hand tools and human labour power alone. A third type are pastoralists who specialise in herding livestock and at the same time may give incidental attention to cultivation of plants. Finally, we may speak of agricultural peoples who are dependent upon a more extensive form of plant cultivation using animal traction or, more recently, tractor power. Here the chief technological symbol is the use of the plough. Such societies depend upon a mixture of plant cultivation and livestock husbandry.

Some anthropologists have made much more of such a classification of societies than may in fact be warranted. For them the significance of this classification is that one may predict from subsistence numerous other strategic characteristics of such societies. Therefore, the classification, it is held, bears out the theoretical orientation of a materialist conception of humans and their culture. This is the view that the subsistence base of a society *determines* the type of social system. This is not the place to enter into a detailed argument concerning this thesis. Yet usage of this classification here, as in many other anthropological works, should not be taken as support for this point of view. The classification is employed because it offers a convenient way of dividing, and so dealing with, a variety of human situations. And like any classification and its implicit theory it bears elements of truth. Thus, we know that practically all hunting-gathering people lack a complex division of labour, social classes, the state and government, and at the other end of the spectrum that practically all agricultural societies have social classes, a complex division of labour, the state and government. It is clear that hunting gathering cannot provide the necessary material wherewithal to sustain such elaborate social systems as can an agricultural system. Thus, hunting-gathering societies are, with only a few exceptions, 'egalitarian' societies in Fried's classification, or 'band type' societies in Service's. And most examples of anarchic polities are likewise to be drawn from hunting-gathering peoples, whilst agricultural societies are almost entirely stratified (Fried) and state type systems where anarchy is at best a marginal occurrence.

As is so true of single factor determinist theories, this one as well, which rests upon material subsistence, has a ring of truth if we remain at the level of certain broad generalities and probabilities. However, such theories break down when we attempt to employ them in explaining the wide variations which occur, for example, within hunting-gathering systems, or the more precise dynamics pertaining to specific aspects of the social order. Nor are they able to explain variations in ideology. Like the geographical environment, mode of subsistence may be said to set limits to what a people by themselves can do and can develop, but within these limits there are, given the inventive genius of the human mind, all kinds of variations which are possible and are not purely epiphenomena of material conditions of life.

Any society at a given time is the product of the collective interaction of its several parts, not of one phenomenon alone. Food gathering of a specific kind is in part a determinant of population size and diversity, as well as of the extent to which sufficient wealth can be produced to allow for certain development in social organisation. Population size and density have much to do with the kinds of social organisation which can appear. For example, a small population can readily sustain a polity based solely upon kinship. At the same time hunting and gathering, like any other mode of subsistence, is also heavily dependent upon the kinds of technology available. Yet the technology and, thus, the whole hunting-gathering base, depends upon the non-material factor of knowledge which is inside people's heads. Knowledge in turn is focussed or oriented by the prevalent kinds of cultural values — what is held to be the important ends of life — and in turn by the existing kinds of technology. In a word the most satisfactory model of a social order may be as an interacting multi-factor system.

The sequence from hunting-gathering through horticulture, pastoralism to agriculture should not be seen as a fixed model of stages of cultural evolution through which every culture must pass, nor should it be viewed as a sequence of ever increasing complexity. It is true that all societies either are, or were once, dependent on hunting-gathering and that most present day agricultural societies started out as hunting-gatherers and evolved into horticulturalists. But there are a variety of other ways or sequences in which societies may develop besides this process. The model of cultural evolution is multilineal, not unilineal.

Regarding degrees of complexity, some hunting-gathering societies are more complex than some horticultural ones, some even more than a few pastoral ones. And some of the horticultural societies are as complex as some of the agricultural ones.

In the descriptions which follow the emphasis will be upon determining patterns and techniques of leadership and mechanisms of social control as indices of anarchic polity. The relations between the sexes and between age groups are two areas of concern to anarchists, and in any modern anarchist theory there is a demand

for full sexual equality and at least an opposition to any irrational
authority over the young. In what follows we will not have a great
deal to say on this subject. The truth is that few societies grant
anything approaching sexual equality and female equality is clearly
not a feature for which most of the societies discussed below are to
be noted.[1] Similarly, the young are invariably subordinate to their
elders and more often than not in an arbitrary manner. We stick
to the strict meaning of anarchy as a polity without rulers, without
government, but again freely admit that this may leave much to
be desired by those who are ideologically anarchists and by others
concerned about liberty as well. Anarchy does not necessarily
mean freedom.

Finally, there is a problem with the names commonly applied to
several of the groups discussed in that they have an ethnocentric
origin. At the same time appropriate alternatives are difficult to
locate. Thus, while Eskimo has its origin in a pejorative, the
alternative, Inuit, which is the name they use for themselves, has
an ethnocentric ring as well. It means people or human beings
carrying with it the implication that outsiders are not human.
Berber is no doubt the most pejorative appelation of all — it
means barbarian. But these people lack a single blanket term for
themselves. Most, however, use some form of Imazighen, that is,
"free men", and I would surmise that none of them would resent
being so called. In this text I have tried to employ neutral terms
for the various groups, but I have not been able to produce any
exhaustive ethnocentric-free list of names. I still use Pygmy for
lack of an alternative and for all I know the names of many groups
may disguise insults of one kind or another. I will use Inuit instead
of Eskimo; San instead of Bushman; Samek instead of Lapp and
Imazighen instead of Berber.

---

[1]A hypothesis developed in the 19th century and in the last decade or so given some
publicity by the Marxist wing of the women's liberation movement, holds that in
the most archaic societies men and women were equal and that the development
of 'property' and agriculture led to male domination. It is certainly true that
there is *greater* equality between the sexes in hunter-gathering societies than in
most agricultural ones. But this 'greater equality' is still within the parameters
of male pre-eminence. Two other notions which frequently appear in conjunction
with that of an ancient sexual equality are the views that the older human society
was matrilineal and that originally something called group marriage was practised.
There is no substantiation for such views in the data of anthropology. Indeed, if
anything, the evidence is against them. Oldest human societies were probably
neither matrilineal nor patrilineal, but rather were bilateral (non-lineal).

III

Anarchy among Hunter-Gatherers

"Among the lessons to be learnt from the life of rude tribes is how society can go on without the policeman to keep order" (Tylor, II, 134).

The hunting-gathering type is obviously the oldest kind of human society, characterising the human way of life from its cultural beginnings and for about 99% of the time thereafter. Beginning about 12,000 years ago, with the invention of plant cultivation and animal husbandry, hunting and gathering began to decline. Today, there is practically no group on earth which relies completely on this way of life. Even the Inuit and Arctic Indians have abandoned full dependence upon hunting and gathering in favour of a livelihood aimed in great part at obtaining furs and manufacturing items for an international luxury market. Elsewhere, the hunter-gatherers such as those to be found in India or in parts of East and Central Africa, are usually specialised castes of professional hunters dependent upon an adjacent agricultural or horticultural society.

Hunter-gatherers constitute simple societies and are primitive in the sense that primitive means that they are more similar to the oldest forms of human society than are other extant ones.[1] But it is an error to conceive of these societies as being the same as those archaic societies. Contemporary hunter-gatherers are present-day people who, like everyone else, have a history; they are not petrified hangovers from a Paleolithic past. They have changed at a different rate than most other people and in different ways. Their

---

[1] Some hunting-gathering societies evolved out of horticultural ones, as for example occurred with several Amazon Forest Indian societies and with some of the Indians of the North American Plains (eg, the Cheyenne).

histories represent various paths of evolutionary development, not necessarily some fixed stage within, or at the bottom of, an evolutionary sequence.

Although hunting-gathering is a type or class of societies, such societies are not undifferentiated, like so many peas in a pod. Contrary to some popular views, there is a considerable variation among them. In delineating the highlights of the type then we should indicate some of the more significant variations.

These societies are dependent upon the acquisition of wild, undomesticated foods: wild game, fish and plants. Nevertheless we find there is some tendency to specialise in exploiting selected resources. Thus, there are those who are largely hunters of sea mammals; others tend more to fishing. There are peoples who may be called big game hunters and those who specialise more in collecting wild seeds. There are also many who are much more omnivorous in their habits.[1]

Reliance upon wild sources of food places greater limits on potential cultural development than any other form of subsistence. There are more severe limits on what a people can do and can invent and utilise when they must rely upon the often precarious and insecure sources offered by nature alone. There is less guarantee as to where the next meal might come from than in an agricultural society. But it is not a life that demands unceasing labour or a kind of bare hand to mouth existence. This is a condition which more appropriately describes a peasantry or 19th century factory working class. Ordinarily hunters and gatherers produce a food supply sufficient for an adequate caloric intake for each member of the group, plus enough for the ritual and ceremonial requirements traditional for the society. Some, chiefly fishing specialists, have been able to build up 'surpluses' and enjoy a more secure food supply than many an agriculturalist. In any event, the parameters of no human society's subsistence are ever so rigid as to preclude freedom in experimentation and innovation.

Hunting-gathering societies invariably have a band type organisation. This means that the basic stable territorial group is a relatively small one, usually under 100 persons. It contains at least a core of individuals who are kinsmen and in most cases all in the band are related to one another. The group is identified with some territory which it, as well as others, sees as belonging to it.

Nomadism is normally a characteristic of such societies. Yet

---

[1]As has already been mentioned, most of these societies no longer exist, but for convenience they will be discussed in the present tense.

this does not mean aimless wandering. Rather there is periodic movement according to some rational plan from one encampment site to another. Nomadism, and especially pedestrian nomadism, inhibits the accumulation of material goods. Nomadic hunters do not make good pack rats since one can hardly carry a mess of junk from one camp to another. A minority of hunting-gathering people have been sedentary, dwelling in villages.

Hunting-gathering societies share a technology based upon the use of stone, wood, bone and ivory tools. They do not of themselves know the art of metallurgy.

There is a minimal social differentiation and specialisation of tasks. The social roles are limited to those of kinship and to roles based on sex and on relative age. The society is characterised by what Radcliffe-Brown referred to as a high degree of substitutability. That is, it is easy to substitute one person for another. One adult male can be fairly readily replaced by another. So each person of the same sex and approximate age is expected to be able to do what any other one in the same category can do. Thus, the adult male is a jack of all trades, or, more correctly, there are no trades. Nevertheless, there are in such societies individuals who do tend to specialise, so that one person may become more adept at fashioning arrow heads than any other in the group and another more knowledgeable in performing rituals or in making cures. Indeed, in some cases the shaman becomes at least a part-time specialist.

Such societies are also egalitarian to the extent that "there are as many positions of prestige in any given age-sex grade as there are persons capable of filling them. . .". At the same time "an egalitarian society does not have any means of fixing or limiting the number of persons capable of executing power" (Fried, 33). Egalitarian does not, however, mean that there is any equality between sexes and between different age groups. In a few hunting-gathering societies, such as the Inuit there is greater equality between the sexes. Nevertheless males are still considered superior.

There are also a few hunting-gathering societies which must be considered as rank societies "in which positions of valued status are somehow limited so that not all those of sufficient talent to occupy such statuses actually achieve them. Such a society may or may not be stratified. That is, a society may sharply limit its positions of prestige without affecting the access of its entire membership to the basic resources upon which life depends" (Fried, 110).

In a classification based on different criteria, Elman Service describes 'chiefdoms' as a type of society with some close parallels

to Fried's rank societies. "Chiefdoms are *redistributional societies*
with a permanent central agency of co-ordination." The central
agency acquires an economic, religious and political role (Service,
1962, 144). The 'redistributor' of communal wealth is a 'chief' or
person in an established position of influence, responsibility and
wealth. The political role of this redistributor or 'chief' varies
considerably. At the anarchic 'pole' we have the examples of the
Yurok and Northwest Coast Indians given below. At the other
extreme there are Polynesian and African chiefs who are in effect
petty kings. Among hunter-gatherers these 'chiefly' or 'rank' style
societies tend to be the wealthiest and economically most secure.

Anarchy is the order of the day among hunter-gatherers. Indeed,
critics will ask why a small face-to-face group needs a government
anyway. And certainly any which may be called fully egalitarian
according to Fried's definition are anarchic.

If this is so we can go further and say that since the egalitarian
hunting-gathering society is the oldest type of human society and
prevailed for the longest period of time — over thousands of
decades — then anarchy must be the oldest and one of the most
enduring kinds of polity. Ten thousand years ago everyone was an
anarchist.

Inuit

Inuit, the indigenous residents of the North American Arctic, are
a well-known people — both in terms of their adaptation to the
hard life of the far north and as participants in an egalitarian
social system. Even Hoebel recognises their "primitive anarchy"
(1954, 67).

Social groupings among Inuit have been referred to as tribes by
some observers, but the term designates a particular geographical
group which shares a common culture and language. It has no
political significance. Birket-Smith writes:

"Thus among the Inuit there is no state which makes use of
their strength, no government to restrict their liberty of action.
If anywhere there exists that community, built upon the basis of
the free accord of free people, of which Kropotkin dreamt, it is
to be found among these poor tribes neighboring upon the North
Pole" (144).

Traditionally Inuit formed local communities or bands which in
some cases consisted of a few dozen members and in others of ten
times that number. In each band there is at least one outstanding
individual and usually one person whom the others recognise as a
'first among equals' (Birket-Smith, 145). Birket-Smith reports that
among the Central Eskimos of the Northern Canadian mainland

this person is called "*isumataq*, he who thinks, the implication being he who thinks for the others" (145). But one might also surmise that the title implies that the person is considered the most intelligent in the group.

In any case, an important basis for leadership is demonstrated ability in activities necessary for survival in this climate: hunting, provision of food and shelter, shrewdness and astuteness. Spencer, describing the North Alaskan Inuit, says that one of the recognised leaders of the community would be a man of wealth — that is, a big boat owner (65). Yet this man has also achieved his position by knowledge and skill in exploiting the local environment.

Aside from such secular leadership, shamans are an important element in Inuit politics as well as religion. A shaman may be a respected hunter, but his power derives from his special relationship with the supernatural forces. The shaman is a curer, a diviner, a conjurer, a magician and a leader in religious ceremony. The Inuit shaman is believed to have the power to ascend into the heavens and descend into the underground, to control weather and other natural phenomena. He can invoke supernatural forces to benefit a person and he can also invoke them to cause injury. Among the Copper Inuit, shamans "held the threat of witchcraft over others and were, for the main part, not highly susceptible to vengeance because of their presumed supernatural immunities" (Damas, 33).

In Inuit society there is no-one who can be called a ruler — a person who can order others to obey him, having behind this order an exclusive right to employ physical force to compel obedience. Leadership is informal and the role of leadership only loosely defined. The commands of a leader can be ignored with impunity, but this could be dangerous, especially in connection with a malevolent shaman. In a community major issues are openly discussed in informal gatherings. Consensus regarding a course of action may result, usually being an approval of the suggestions made by influential men. However, if unanimity of opinion is not forthcoming, the disagreeing parties may merely go their own way.

The Inuit case points to the potential pitfalls of a system in which there is no formal leadership and where anarchy prevails. As we have noted, a shaman can exert considerable power by inducing fear of his supernatural powers, so that he could enhance his position, although he would not thereby enhance his prestige. Damas says they were more feared than respected (33).

A related problem which arises in Inuit society is the man who chooses to reject community morality and assert his personal strength in acquiring whatever he wanted. Often such men are able to run roughshod over others in a community, but inevitably must ultimately come to a violent demise themselves. They might be dispatched by a revenge killing. Or in vigilante fashion, a number of men, sometimes the offender's relatives, would plan the execution. A less permanent solution is to drive the individual out of the group. In any case some form of diffuse sanction is the only means employed to overcome such threats.

All forms of leadership, including that of shaman, are achieved statuses in Inuit society. As one earns status, so one might also lose it. Loss of position could come with the appearance of what is recognised as a better leader, hunter or shaman or as a result of the failure of shamanic powers.

Alleged wrong-doers could be ostracised and in some cases driven out of the village, or, as we have already mentioned, in extreme cases they might be killed. Gossip and argument are effective techniques for lesser offences. Occasionally a severe crime might go entirely unpunished. Ordinarily the kinsman of a murdered man sought revenge and feuds of a limited sort have not been unknown. Inuit frequently settle disputes through competitive trials between opponents, with the audience deciding who is victorious and therefore winner in the dispute. Two disputants might therefore engage in a wrestling match, or they might compete with one another in composing songs which, among other things, attempt to outdo each other in insult. Shamans contest with each other by demonstrating their marvellous powers in grand spectacles which could be the highlight of an otherwise dreary and dark winter.

An Inuit woman could not be considered as fully equal to a man, yet she has a liberty and influence which exceeds that of women in most other societies. It is sometimes argued that the high position of Inuit women results from their crucial role in the economy. An adult male Inuit requires assistance in maintaining a household; he cannot survive without an adult female fulfilling her role. So necessary are women to the household that if a man is unable to find a single woman to take as his wife, he may even indulge in polyandry and marry a woman who already has a husband. It is true that in a difficult land, such as the Arctic, one would expect the co-operative interdependence of a family group to have greater significance than it might under less severe conditions. Thus the economic importance of the woman's role elevates her status in such a society. On the other hand, among hunters and gatherers elsewhere women are known to provide over 50% of the food supply in their gathering activities, in addition to filling other crucial economic roles in society. Yet these women do not have the freedom or equality of their Inuit counterparts. The Australian Aboriginals are a case in point. Inuit may well award women more equality and freedom in part because of their important economic role, but, in fact, the position of these women derives mostly from an emphasis upon self-reliance which is instilled in every Inuit. A self-reliant person must be given a greater degree of freedom. This emphasis also, I think, helps explain why children in Inuit society are treated as distinct persons with specific inalienable rights. In contrast, many other peoples see children at best as mere extensions of the person of their father. Again, in the environment of the Inuit, co-operative activity is crucial, but self-reliance, learning to get along on your own, is mandatory if one is to survive.

San

In the arid zones of southern Africa there are peoples collectively referred to as Bushmen or by their close relatives, the Hottentots, as San. Most of them have long since abandoned a hunting-gathering way of life to become employed as servants by neighboring Negroid groups or European farmers. A small handful, numbering in the hundreds, have at least up until a scant few years ago persisted in the old traditions in the refuge of the desert areas of Botswana and Namibia.

The San are organized into bands or camps which are loosely structured groups composed primarily of related individuals (often patrilineally related to a common male ancestor) and dwelling in a territory identified with the band.

San have no formal leaders, neither headmen nor chiefs, but bands do have leaders or persons of influence. These are invariably "owners" of the lands which surround a water hole and represent the band territory or the area which provides its general needs. "Owners" comprise the core of related persons, usually siblings or cousins, in the band who have lived around its water hole longer than anyone else and are therefore recognized as collective owners, as "hosts" of the territory to whom anyone from outside the group is expected to request permission on visiting the area. This kind of ownership passes from one generation to the next as long as any descendents remain within it.

One who is not an "owner" may seek to achieve leadership status by marrying a woman in another band who is an owner. Yet ownership alone is insufficient to place one in the forefront. Other attributes of leadership include being the older within a large family with many children and grandchildren. Moreover one should possess several personal qualities. Thus, one who is a powerful speaker is respected. It helps also to be recognized as a mood mediator. Under no circumstances should a leader be "arrogant, overbearing, boastful, or aloof." (Lee, 345). Lee notes that these characteristics of the leader are also stressed among Australian aboriginals.

Camp leaders are preeminent in decision making, mediation and food distribution. Yet one !Kung San in response to a question as to whether his group had headmen replied: "Of course we have headmen! In fact we are all headmen . . . each one of us is headman over himself" (Lee, 348).

Another more recent kind of leader has arisen among Bushmen as a consequence of contact with neighboring Blacks, peoples who have a more hierarchical social system. Such leaders are brokers or liaison agents with the outside non-San peoples and have their position because of their ability to deal with foreigners and carry on entrepreneurial affairs. Such individuals are rarely camp or community leaders.

There are also medicine men whose sole role is the curing of illness, receiving no special privilege because of this position. The San lack sorcerers and witches. Throughout the society men are dominant, a factor Marshall attributes partly to their superior physical strength, but also to their prestige role as hunters and thus as those who provide the meat for the community (despite the fact that plants collected by women supply the bulk of the food). Lee, however, has noted that some women become recognized camp leaders.

San fear fighting and desire to avoid all hostility. At the same time fights do arise and sometimes lead to killing. Most conflicts are in the nature of verbal abuse and argument relating to food and gift distribution or accusations of laziness and stinginess. When actual physical combat is provoked those around the combatants, most often close kin or supporters of one of the protagonists, immediately seek to separate the participants and to pacify them. Extended discussion may ensue but the antagonists remain silent. "The trance dance that sometimes follows a fight may serve as a peace-making mechanism when trance performers give ritual healing to persons on both sides of the argument" (Lee, 377). It is considered particularly important to intervene in a fight involving men between ages 20 and 50 since they have a monopoly on the poisoned arrows. Thus were they to lose all self control — and physical combat among these people is likened to a state of temporary insanity — someone would surely die.

Although San do not engage in ritual murder or sacrifice they sometimes carry out revenge killings. Yet even these may be avoided for fear of escalating the violence. On some occasions killers have been "executed" through the mutual agreement of a group of men. According to Lee a goodly number of those who are killed in fights are non-combatants, being usually persons who seek to intervene to stop a fight or occasionally a by-stander. Any severe conflict is usually resolved by the group splitting up.

According to Lee a camp persists as long as food is shared amongst its members, but once this is discontinued the group ceases to exist. There are specific rules concerning the distribution of wild game. The bulk of any kill must be distributed initially by its 'owner', the man who owns the arrow which first entered the animal. So a hunter who shoots an arrow loaned to him by another is merely shooting for that person. Meat is first distributed amongst a small group, including the hunters and the owner of the arrow. This group in turn distributes portions to a wider circle of individuals and they to still a larger group. Consequently, members of the sharing group are involved in a reciprocity system which obligates those who receive to return gifts of meat in future distributions.

Because groups are small, nearly all social relations are actually guided in terms of kinship concepts. There is no organisation or integration of San beyond the band level. One retains band membership throughout life, along with the associated rights to its resources. Yet members do leave their home band and join others. They may still return at a future date.

Children are treated permissively by parents. Marshall affirms the latter are especially fond of younger children and gentle in their treatment of them. "!Kung children are never harshly punished. One father said that if he had a boy who was quarrelsome or who disobeyed the rules — for instance, the absolute rule of the !Kung against stealing food or possessions — what he would do about it would be to keep the boy right with him until he learned sense. The children on their part do not often do things that call for punishment. They usually fall in with group life and do what is expected of them without apparent uncertainty, frustration, or fear; and expressions of resistance or hostility towards their parents, the group, or each other are very much the exception" (Marshall, 264).

Pygmies
The traditional Pygmy hunters dwell in the rain forests of the interior of Zaire living in small nomadic bands. There is neither formalised leadership nor are there formal group councils, although outstanding men and women are recognised in each band. No-one,

however, wishes to take it upon himself to make judgments or impose punishments on others. Rather, the maintainance of order is a co-operative affair, or something left up to supernatural forces. ". . . Pygmies dislike and avoid personal authority", says Turnbull, "though they are by no means devoid of a sense of responsibility. It is rather that they think of responsibility as communal" (1962, 125). The Pygmies told Turnbull they had no leaders, lawmakers or government "because we are the people of the forest"; the forest "is the chief, the lawgiver, the leader, the final arbitrator" (1962, 126).

When a theft has occurred there is a detailed discussion of the case by an assembly of the whole encampment. When consensus has been reached as to the guilty party, all those who feel so inclined collectively administer a sound thrashing to the offender. The most outrageous offences, it is believed, are so terrible that they result in supernatural punishment. Minor disputes and alleged offences are often left to the litigants who either settle them through argument or a mild fight. Such encounters may, however, escalate and soon the whole band may be involved in arguing the case. Turnbull writes that if you lose patience with your wife's nagging, you call on your friends to assist you in trying to put her in her place. Your wife will do the same, so that the entire camp is drawn into the argument. "At this point someone — very often an older person with too many relatives and friends to be accused of being partisan — steps in with the familiar remark that everyone is making too much noise, or else diverts the issue onto a totally different track so that people forget the origin of the argument and give it up" (1962, 124).

Other techniques of diffuse sanctions employed commonly by Pygmies include the use of ostracism and ridicule. In most bands there is a young bachelor with some repute as a hunter. He assumes the role of the clown and lampoons the disputants in a conflict.

The process of decision-making in everyday community affairs is similar to the technique for dealing with disputes. Affairs are dealt with in a casual and informal way and without the appearance of individual leadership. In deciding on a hunt, each adult male is involved in discussion until agreement is reached. Women, too, participate by offering their opinions.

Pygmy society is strongly communal in its orientation and the emphasis on co-operative action is such that when compared to the Inuit these Arctic dwellers seem very individualistic indeed. Pygmies probably approach the anarchist ideal more closely than most other groups. While others have the form of anarchy, Pygmies appear to have captured some of the spirit as well.

There is an attempt to avoid leadership by one or a few, to arrive at decisions by full communal participation and consensus. Pygmies, like the Inuit, minimise discrimination based upon sex and age differences.

Australian hunters and foragers

Australian society, like that of other hunters, is organised on a band basis. Several families traditionally hunted and camped together and claimed a territory for economic exploitation and as a ritual and totemic centre. These families were related and for the most part through the male line, usually to a common paternal grandfather or great grandfather.

Australians have often been described as the most primitive people in the world — or as having the simplest culture. But such descriptions contribute more to confusion and misunderstanding of Australian cultures than they do to clarification. It is true that few people known to modern society have possessed a more rudimentary and limited technology. An Australian could readily carry all his earthly possessions under his arm. Spears and throwing sticks were his most elaborate form of projectile; he did not know the use or manufacture of the bow and arrow. In technology Australians did not elaborate on a wide range of different types of tools, rather they concentrated on the development of a great many styles within a few kinds of tools. Thus, one finds a wide variety of throwing sticks or of spears.

Similarly Australians did not experiment with many different social structures; their social organisation was based on the single principle of kinship. Yet, they managed to invent a variety of kinship structures. Indeed, they played upon a single theme — that of dual division — in such a way as to create several complex kinship patterns. The most elementary form of dual division is to cut a society into two groups (moieties) which engage in mutual exchange, including the exchange of women, so that wives are derived from the opposite group. Australians elaborated this dual principle so as to create four and eight 'section' systems which determined incest rules and the persons whom one might marry. To the outsider, such as the introductory anthropology student, these systems become extremely complex conundrums. Australian mythology and ceremony and their attendant art forms are similarly by no means simple or crude. On the contrary, they must be recognised as rich and highly developed. In sum, Australians seem to have taken a minimum number of simple principles and woven them into a complex web of variant patterns. Further, they seem to have been highly concerned with the realms of kinship, mythology and ceremonial and uninterested in technology. In contrast, western society has been interested primarily in the latter while innovation in kinship and ceremonial verges on being tabooed. Thus arises the misleading notion that Australians are 'primitive' (in a pejorative sense), crude and simple.

Australian political organisation requires no complexity and it has none. Their political system has been called a 'gerontocracy' — by which is meant a rule by old men. More correctly, for Australia it means that older men are the most influential and their opinions are accepted because of the prestige of their elderly positions. Further, one's elders are one's grandfathers, so there is the moral force of kinship behind their words. One accepts the decision of the elder males also out of fear of public opinion, believing all others in the band would disapprove of any dissent. Further, older men are considered to have a certain sanctity, since it is they who are the repositories of all the sacred wisdom of the group. Among the Murngin, for example, each clan has ceremonial leaders who know all the rituals of that clan. The position is inherited from father to son. By control of the ceremonial system these leaders also control who may be initiated into which ceremonies and at which time. This is extremely crucial to the Murngin male, who, in order to be a fully fledged member of society, must in the course of his life pass through several rites of passage from one age group to another. These rites reveal knowledge which is held to be necessary to group survival. Life is a process of being initiated into various ceremonies and, thus, secrets of life, and its climax is the ultimate initiation into "the final mysteries of life by seeing the most esoteric of the totems" (Warner, 132). The main force available to the elders, then, appears to be a supernatural sanction: the threat of withholding admission to certain knowledge deemed essential to success in life. Additionally, elders may turn public opinion against a person.

Within a band the elders are the ones concerned with dealing with strangers and the ones responsible for organising blood feuds or instigating others to impose a punishment on malefactors. Elders, however, have no power as a police force to enforce law. They can only encourage physically stronger men in the community to try to impose a punishment on an alleged culprit.

Supernatural sanctions form an important part of the Australian's techniques to maintain order. Bone pointing is well known and one does not have to be a particular specialist in order to use it. In this technique a magic bone is pointed in the direction of one's enemy, who is, of course, informed that this has been done. Consequently the victim is supposed to become ill and die. As Cannon long ago pointed out, this technique does achieve results. Victims appear to die because they simply resign themselves to death.

Like the Inuit the Australians have part-time religious specialists or shamans. These undergo special initiations, often under the direction of a group of shamans who constitute a kind of rudimentary guild of craft specialists. Shamans have the power to counteract the magic of an enemy. They can also destroy another man. Thus they are a major force for mobilising and influencing public opinion and, according to Warner, they are as effective in this respect as ceremonial leaders (242).

Australian society represents a political system with somewhat more structure and formality than characterised the Inuit and Pygmy. Indeed, gerontocratic features are more common to African horticulturalists. Australians, nevertheless, function according to diffuse and religious sanctions. The control by the older men of access to those ceremonial initiations deemed essential for attaining full male status, approaches a rudimentary government. Yet since Australian groups are communities of kinsmen and these elders are kinsmen, addressed and treated as such, their position is more clearly that of grandfather than that of governor or policeman. In addition, elders in no way have any monopoly on the uses of violence to impose their commands and this, of course, is the keystone of a governmental structure.

Other hunter-gatherers

One could continue with a catalogue of most hunting-gathering societies as societies without government. For the most part they follow the pattern characteristic of the foregoing peoples: leadership is informal and largely achieved; it may be invested in technicians such as the good hunter among the Inuit or Northern Athabaskan Indians, or in the shaman, or, as in Australia, ascribed to the older men of the community; rules are enforced through diffuse and religious sanctions and egalitarianism, at least within a given age-sex group, prevails.

Some hunters and gatherers have the rudiments of governmental forms, such as the warrior societies among Plains Indians. Others are 'ranked' societies, which nevertheless have the characteristics of functioning anarchies. The Indians of central and northern California had a very simple rank system, while those of the Northwest Coast had a complex one.

The Yurok

Of the Californians let us briefly consider the Yurok. They were fishermen and seed (acorn) gatherers as well as hunters. The Yurok constitute small rather permanent communities composed of patrilineally related families centred around a senior male — 'the rich man'. The 'rich man' office is essentially the senior rank in the community. Its holder is overseer of the group's wealth. He directs activities at salmon weirs and on acorn grounds and could draw upon the wealth of the community to pay bride wealth or blood money. He maintains his position through his 'influence' and displays characteristics deemed proper for a Yurok man of prestige, particularly through demonstrations of his great generosity and, hence, wealth. Any decisions he might make could only be enforced by withholding his generosity or threatening to do so. Obviously, he could do greater favours for those whom he saw as the most obedient and loyal.

The Yurok possess an elaborate set of regulations concerning offences, but the technique employed to enforce these rules is not one of law enforcement, but rather one of mediation. Disputants in a case choose 'go betweens' or 'crosses' who cross back and forth between the conflicting sides carrying offers and counter offers until an agreement is reached. The go-betweens are expected to be completely impartial and to bring forth an agreement which is fair to both sides. They gather the evidence and make a judgment about damages on the basis of a scale which forms part of Yurok traditional regulations. Individuals judged as offenders by the go-betweens are expected to pay fines in accord with these regulations. Thus a man's life is valued as equal to the bride wealth paid for his mother.

Hoebel considers that these circumstances constitute a court of law (1961, 25). However, Kroeber clearly indicates that the opposing parties involved have to *agree* to the decision of the crosses (1953). They are therefore not judges with the power to compel obedience by force. They are negotiators with the moral backing of society. This is a kind of non-governmental system of dispute settlement which one finds widely dispersed throughout the world and one which we will encounter again in the descriptions to follow. That it is so common and widespread may indicate that it has proven a most successful mechanism for maintaining peace. It should be noted that the main aim of this form of justice is not to assess guilt and gloat over rights and wrongs, but rather it is to re-establish communal peace and group harmony.

Yurok depend upon other important devices such as gossip and sometimes 'rash youths' attempt to form a kind of vigilante committee to settle disputes, thus transforming a minor issue into a major conflict and possibly a blood feud.

Northwest Coast Indians

In the Northwest Coast of America, the Indians developed one of the most elaborate cultures known for a hunting-gathering people. It was based largely upon fishing and whaling. These people were the great potlatch givers. They developed a complex ceremonial system of gift giving and partying by which individuals sought to outdo and so shame or 'flatten' others by their generosity. Through potlatching one could earn various named and privileged ranks. Thus society was divided into three groups: those who held one or more ranks; freemen who held no rank but who were kinsmen of those who did and were expected to assist in amassing wealth for potlatch party engagements; and, finally, at the bottom there were slaves. These were persons captured in warfare or others given to pay damages for an offence. This ranking system should not be confused with a class system. Ranking involves differential status of individuals; class involves differential status of groups. Thus among the Northwest Coast Indians a man might acquire many titles and be of highest rank. Yet other members of his family might well not have this status at all. An eldest son would inherit 'nobility' from his father, while the youngest son was little more than a commoner.

There are differences in wealth and sharp competitions for prestige and for the limited number of ranked positions. Yet the competition involved has sometimes been misunderstood as some flagrant, individualistic form which would be dear to the heart of the *laissez faire* capitalist. Actually, that which existed between rank holders vying for yet more exalted positions depended upon wealth which was provided by the co-operative group activity of the kinsmen of the rank holder. If competition existed at all levels of the system it would have been totally unworkable. This is something few of those who worship at the altar of competition see, namely, that co-operation is fundamental to all human activity, even to being able to compete.

The man with the highest rank in a village is often referred to as the 'chief'. However, as in other instances of this kind, this usage is misleading. A senior ranked 'noble' was called a chief because he was senior and consequently had privileges which were not shared with others. Thus among the Nootka the chief or senior 'noble' of several local settlements had certain prior rights to the salmon streams and ocean waters for fish and sea mammals; he owned important root and berry patches and the salvage materials which landed on the shores of his territory.

The chief was expected to demonstrate liberality, generosity and leadership. Yet he had little or no authority to impose his will by force. He was not a chief in the sense of executive officer with police powers.

Among the Carrier of the British Columbia interior, when families quarrelled the 'chief' called all the people to his house where he covered "his head with swan's down, the time honored symbol of peace, and dance(d) before them to the chanting of his personal song and the shaking of his rattle". After the dance he delivered an oration on the wealth he and his clan-phratry had expended to get titles. He exhorted the disputants to settle their quarrel and warned of the troubles which would come if it continued (Jenness, 518). This was the limit of his contribution to settling disputes. The phratry chief among the Carrier ordered murderers to fast for twenty-five days and he presided at a ceremony in which the murderer and his clan's people handed over a blood price.

Writing of the West Coast Indians in general, Drucker reports that "in the rare instances when blood was shed" within a kin group "usually nothing was done" since the group could not take revenge upon itself or pay itself blood money (1965, 74). Revenge was resorted to when a person of one kin group murdered one in another. Among most of the Coastal people (except for the Kwakiutl and Nootka) the alternative to a revenge attack in the case of intergroup murder was for one person from the offending group to be asked to "come forth voluntarily to be slain". Witches accused of practising black magic were often slain and these killings weng unavenged.

Northwest Coast societies seem to represent cases of marginal anarchy, where the 'chiefs' or 'nobles', as men of clear rank and privilege, held more 'legitimate' authority than others. Yet the situation was still sufficiently ambiguous for such chiefs to have no monopoly of force and most social control mechanisms were clearly of a diffuse or religious nature.

Bibliographic note
Inuit data are derived from Birket-Smith, Damas and Spencer (see Bibliography). San materials are from Lee, Marshall and Thomas. Turnbull is the source for the Pygmies while Elkin, Sharp, Spencer and Gillin, and Warner are the main sources for the Australians. The Northwest Coast description is from Drucker and Jenness while that on the Californians is from Kroeber. For other American Indian groups see Hallowell for Ojibwa and Honigmann for Northern Athabascans.

IV

Anarchist Gardeners

Horticultural societies depend primarily upon gardening activity for food supply. This differs from agriculture which entails extensive cultivation employing animal or mechanical draft power in cultivating large fields. In horticulture only human labour is used and the digging stick or hoe is the chief implement rather than the plough. Horticultural peoples practice slash and burn, or shifting cultivation, in which an area is burned over and cleared of brush and forest. Then the field is planted year after year until the unfertilised soil no longer yields a good crop, at which time the place is abandoned and the gardeners shift to another one. This means that although horticulturalists are ordinarily a sedentary people, especially compared to most hunter-gatherers, they are occasionally forced to move their dwellings and villages in order to be near their gardens.

Horticulturalists usually specialise in a limited number of crops. In North America there was a corn, beans and squash complex; New Guineans rely upon a considerable variety of different kinds of yams. Garden foods are often supplemented by resorting to hunting and gathering activities, which in some cases provide as much as the gardens themselves. Another food source is domesticated animals. New Guineans, particularly, spend great energy and time in swine husbandry; roast pork is central to any feast or ceremony. In Sub-Saharan Africa, gardeners often keep cattle, sheep and goats. Among American Indians, however, animal husbandry was never of any importance and practically all their animal protein was derived from wild game.

This kind of subsistence provides a platform for launching a variety of cultural innovations not found among hunter-gatherers. Some African horticulturalists were able to develop stratified, class-based societies with specialised craftsmen and full-time religious specialists, all on the basis of highly productive gardens cultivated by the use of the iron hoe. In America, the Aztecs, Mayans and Incas did the same without metal implements. In both areas there was a relatively heavy density of population and in West Africa this entailed the development of cities as well. Enduring, aggressive empire states arose and fell and true warfare was common.

For the most part, however, horticultural societies remain with a simple division of labour according to age and sex. Although some, such as in Polynesia, evolved formal ranks and chiefs or rulers, probably the majority are 'egalitarian'. A great many horticultural societies would fall into Service's 'tribal' type. The tribe is "a body of people of common derivation and custom, in possession and control of their own extensive territory. But if in some degree socially articulated, a tribe is specifically unlike a modern nation in that its several communities are not united under a sovereign governing authority, nor are the boundaries of the whole thus clearly and politically determined. The tribe builds itself up from within, the smaller community segments joined in groups of higher order, yet just where it becomes greatest the structure becomes weakest: the tribe as such is the most tenuous of arrangements, without even a semblance of collective organisation. The tribe is also uncomplicated in another way. Its economics, its politics, its religion are not conducted by different institutions specifically designed for the purpose but coincidentally by the same kinship and local groups: the lineage and clan segments of the tribe, the households and villages, which thus appear as versatile organisations in charge of the entire social life". This is a decentralised, functionally generalised, and segmentary society (Sahlins, 1968, viii). Most of the horticultural societies having anarchic characteristics are tribal and egalitarian societies. Yet some are ranked societies, as Fried would call them, or 'chiefdoms' in Service's language.

Examples of anarchic horticulturalists can readily be drawn from Africa, Southeast Asia and South America. Sub-Saharan Africa provides numerous cases of anarchic polities organised along tribal lines as defined above. Most New Guinea societies are also cases of functioning anarchy, but here the social organisation, though basically of the chiefdom type, has certain 'tribal' characteristics as well.

Sub-Saharan Africa
Scattered throughout the continent south of the Sahara are dozens

of anarchic societies, some of which are the most populous of all anarchic communities. For horticultural people the main concentration is the Volta River area of West Africa, the plateau of central Nigeria and a band across mid-Africa just north of the equator. A few are found in southern Africa while a major concentration is among pastoral peoples of East Africa (see Chapter V).

The anarchic horticultural societies of Africa are primarily limited to the more equatorial zone of the continent — the area of greater forestation and rainfall. The savannah grasslands to the north have proven more amenable to the establishment and expansion of empire states. Here in the open country, free of tsetse fly infestation one can better keep cavalry and deploy them as devices for domination. Closer to the equator, savannah gives way to dense forest and eventually to tropical rain forest, neither of which are suitable for horse keeping and in both of which it is easier to conduct defensive warfare with bows and arrows — the 'democratic' weapon of warfare since anyone can have one. Thus, anarchic systems have been able to survive until recently adjacent to predatory states (Goody, 1971).

African anarchic polities are invariably characterised by the presence of slavery and sometimes of debased pariah castes. Neither include very large numbers, nor are they of much importance in the total social system. Slaves are mostly war captives and pawns and there is little slave trading. Nevertheless, these institutions along with the normal inferior position of women and prevalence of patriarchal authority hardly make such polities oases of freedom, even though they may have no government or state. Africa affords, in its myriad of anarchic and near anarchic societies, innumerable cases of transition between anarchy and archy. Especially important for the rise of the state and decline of anarchy in many of these societies is the role of secret societies and of age grading. In West Africa secret societies are important. They may be voluntary organisations or ones designed to initiate the entire adult male population. A major part of their function is to enforce community rules and punish those believed to be wrong doers. This then represents, depending on one's point of view, a kind of institutionalised vigilante committee, or a rudimentary police force. In the case of the Ibo who are discussed below, the age grades assume a governmental function in an otherwise anarchic polity. Part of the responsibility of those initiated into the younger grade is to act as policemen and enforce the rulings of the village courts which are presided over by members of the middle age grade.

Lugbara

Over a third of a million Lugbara dwell in southern Uganda and
northern Zaire. As horticulturalists they grow chiefly eleusine and
sorghum, but they also keep some cattle. The Lugbara live on open
rolling plains in a highland area of 4-5,000 feet elevation. They, like
their neighbours, are politically decentralised, traditionally having
no chiefs and the fundamental form of social organisation is the
segmentary lineage.[1]

The basic social grouping is the family, either some type of
joint family or a nuclear group. Families related through males
and dwelling in a neighbourhood comprise a 'family cluster' or
minimal lineage of three to four generations depth. The cluster
might also include individuals who are not members of the lineage
group, such as a sister's son or daughter's husband. It might also
have 'clients' residing within it. These are persons who escaped
from their own homes in times of war or famine, or who had been
expelled for some offence. Except for those clients who had not
married into the cluster, the residents are subject to the elder of
the group, who is its genealogically senior member. His authority

---

[1]The classical conception of the segmentary lineage system as outlined by E. E.
Evans-Pritchard in *The Nuer*, and as reflected in Middleton's description of the
Lugbara has been subjected to considerable criticism over the last several years.
The criticism stresses the following points:
(1) Segmentary "theory" alleges that in a segmentary lineage system any important
social and political relations are explicable in terms of lineage affiliation.
Cleavages, alliances, feuds, mutual aid are all determined by lineage affiliation.
This emphasis overlooks other types of social relationships which can be equally
important and often override an individual's or group's lineage obligations.
These relationships include community membership, friendship, neighborhood
and affinal ties, relationships with one's mother's kin, and relationships of work
and economic enterprise. Lineages, then, are not the solidary, close knit corporate
bodies claimed by the theory.
(2) In segmentary "theory" it is held that opposition arises between segments
of the same level, that is, a major lineage opposes another major lineage but
never a minor or minimal lineage. The theory also argues that the complementary
segments are approximately equal in strength. But there are too many exceptions
to these points, especially to the latter, for them to be accepted as invariable
characteristics of the segmentary lineage.
(3) Presumably membership in a lineage within the segmentary system is based
exclusively upon kin ties through males and to a common male ancestor. In fact,
there is often manipulation and jockeying with genealogies so that some individuals
who are not so related are absorbed into the lineage. Aside from these kinds of
fictions, the alleged common male ancestor is sometimes also only an invention.
In sum we may say that the segmentary "theory" presents a people's ideology
about their social system, an ideology which is only imperfectly reflected in their
everyday life and which therefore clearly tells only a biased story.

is primarily ritual in that he can invoke the ancestral ghosts, who have influence only on their descendents.

The lineage owns the territory within which its members reside and the elder allocates use rights within it as well as the rights to its resources, including daughters of the lineage. Further, he is in control of the use of livestock. Within the minimal lineage the elder is responsible for settling disputes. He may also initiate hostile relations with other groups.

Related minimal lineages form yet another lineage segment (minor lineage), which in turn is consolidated into larger segments (major lineages) and these in turn constitute sub clans which consolidate to form clans. However, the number of levels of segmentation among the Lugbara varies. The following diagram of the levels of segmentation within a Lugbara tribe shows on the right side the various segments as territorial units, beginning at the lowest level of the family cluster and culminating in the subtribe. On the left side of the diagram is the segmentary system in terms of descent groups, commencing with the smallest segment, the minimal lineage, whose personnel is roughly equivalent to the territorial unit, the family cluster. (It will be recalled that some residents of the family cluster are not agnatic kinsmen.) Correspondingly each higher level of segmentation of the descent groups has an approximate correspondence to equivalent levels of territorial groups. Again, the rough correspondence results from the fact that while territories are identified with a given descent group, they may include residents not belonging to that descent group.

The Segments of a Lugbara Tribe:

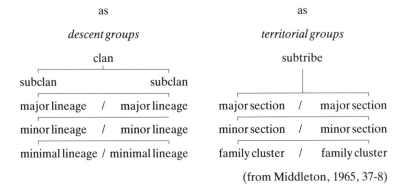

(from Middleton, 1965, 37-8)

The major lineage comprises a most strategic segment within Lugbara society since it is within this group that marriage and fratricide are prohibited and kinship terms are used as forms of address. The major lineage is the feud unit: the body that presumably unites to engage in hostilities against other equivalent segments and within which feuding is not supposed to occur, although it does occasionally.

Within the minor lineage only fighting with sticks and fists is permitted: no bows and arrows or spears can be used since there is no technique, ritual or otherwise, by which the group can deal with the fratricide which might result. We have encountered this notion before: that fratricide, that is, murder carried out within a closely related group, is so horrendous that the community has no established means to deal with it. Nevertheless, a Lugbara killer would marry his victim's widows and donate a bull to the victim's mother's brother, but still this does not repair the injury done. A killing between minor segments of the same lineage is also a heinous deed, but compensation in the form of cattle is considered payable to re-establish group harmony. A homicide involving two major lineages entails no compensation, but rather retaliation may be resorted to. Such fighting can go on between groups for some time. Eventually, when everyone gets tired of hostilities, elders from both sides, in addition to elders from related but uninvolved lineages, gather and negotiate a peace. Should the parties continue to fight the elders may invoke a collective curse upon them. In the curse those ancestral ghosts common to the conflicting parties are asked to bring sickness upon all those who disobey.

Killings within a tribe and between its subclans are compensated for, but beyond this level there is no compensation and the fighting that goes on between tribes continues until third parties are able to intervene successfully, or until the matter is forgotten.

As is usual in other systems of this sort, the most intense feelings of identification, and the most active functioning in terms of mutual interrelationship, is at the minimal level. This gradually decreases as one ascends to encompass larger and larger groups and numbers of people, until one can say that the tribal level has little or no significance. Nevertheless, all Lugbara have the *belief* that they are all kin. They express their own social relations by speaking of groups which are *juru*, wherein potentially hostile relations obtain, and those which are *o'dipi*, which include all those within a group's direct social relations which are not *juru*. Ordinarily *o'dipi* refers to the agnatic descendants of a common ancestor, often a man's major lineage. Thus, as with the latter, among *o'dipi* there is supposed to be no fighting, no intermarriage and any girl is called 'sister'. At any given time a group may be regarded as *juru* and later it may become *o'dipi*.

The chief form of sanction in Lugbara society is religious. Ancestral ghosts may themselves directly impose their vengeance through sickness. Otherwise the elder may invoke the power of the ghosts against individuals, including his own dependants within the family cluster. The power of the ghost invocation by an elder extends as far as there are common ghosts. Non-agnatic kin may curse one another for breaches of kinship ties. Witchcraft accusations are directed against neighbours. Within the community of kin and neighbours, order is maintained through these several supernatural sanctions, all of which form a single mystical system.

The rainmaker is a powerful figure in Lugbara society, as he is in many neighbouring groups. Among the northern Lugbara, where he is the senior member of the senior line of the senior major lineage of a subclan, he is able to bring an end to hostilities by calling people together to prohibit fighting on pain of his cursing those who do not obey. In some areas wrongdoers may find a sanctuary in his person.

Other important men in Lugbara society are 'men whose names are known'. These are invariably wealthy men, but they also have admirable character and thus attract a following. Their influence may spread over several tribes and their status is neither attached to the lineage system nor is it hereditary. They carry white staves as symbols of their position. Like the rainmakers they can curse combatants in a feud and may act as a sanctuary for a refugee and as a mediator in quarrels. For a short period, first in 1895 and again in 1910 'prophets' appeared among the Lugbara and had some influence.

The Lugbara have unmistakable anarchic characteristics. Yet there exist certain specific kinds of persons — rainmakers and 'men whose names are known' — who have a superior cursing power which sets them off as privileged individuals. Here we have the beginning of a proto-governmental structure.

Konkomba
The Konkomba number about 50,000 people and reside in northern Togo where they are chiefly grain farmers raising sorghum, millet and yams. They have a typically African segmentary lineage system based on patrilineal descent (cf, Lugbara example). Konkombaland is divided into several tribes each of which in turn segment into several clans. Each clan rarely has more than 250 members and

is the basic unit occupying, and being identified with, a specific
territory that is its own. Clans divide into two or more lineages.

The oldest man in a lineage is its head, while the clan head is
the senior of all the several lineage heads. Mutual assistance in
work occurs within the clan and more commonly among members
of the lineage segment of the clan. The clan is also a church
or a parish of the prevailing fertility religion, the members of
which are responsible for major rituals associated with sowing
and offerings to the sacred land. Not only is the clan defined by
economic, religious and kinship functions, but it is the primary
mechanism of social control. Within the clan, disputes are to
be settled by mediation and no violence is tolerated. Disputes
with individuals outside the clan require no obligatory arbitration
and one may resort to force or threat of retaliation. Within the
clan the elder demands observance of the rules, but he has no
power to enforce his decisions. The power he has is of a ritual
and moral nature rather than judicial. As the chief and oldest
kinsman his fellow clansmen owe him a moral obligation which
is reinforced by the fact that as the eldest he is nearest the sacred
ancestors. In addition he is guardian of the land. Within the clan,
infractions are dealt with by ostracising a culprit, or by assessment
of fines. For the latter there is no means to compel payment,
aside from the expression of disapproval by fellow clansmen and
the feeling of a moral-ritual obligation to conform. We must
appreciate, however, that in a small closely-knit community,
in which everyone 'believes' and where there are no cynics or
atheists, such sanctions are extremely powerful. As was noted
with the Pygmies, the most horrendous crimes are not punished
by men at all, so with the Konkomba, if a man kills a fellow
clansman he would himself die. "God", say the Konkomba, "will
not suffer to live one who has killed his brother and there is no
ritual or medicinal protection for the fratricide" (Tait, 1950, 275).
Tait, however, believes that murder of fellow clansmen does not
actually occur.

Aside from the elders within a clan, another man of influence is
the diviner, who may build up a reputation which extends over a
wide area.

Ordinarily the relationship between clans is one of relative
hostility, but those which are neighbours and others which may
co-operate in ritual affairs have harmonious relations. Such groups
do not feud, especially those with close ritual ties. Clans which
have, or claim to have, a near kinship relation are also not
supposed to indulge in feuds. Nevertheless, Tait reports two
closely-related clans whose feuding with one another was so

notorious that it was widely remembered among Konkomba 30 years later.

Clans within the same tribe which engage in feud may formally end hostilities by negotiation and ritual burial of the arrows of war. But feuds between clans of different tribes are 'endless' and there appear to be no formal means to bring peace. Apparently, those involved might eventually get tired of fighting.

The tribe among the Konkomba is an amorphous entity. It has a name and is associated with a territory in that it is the sum of the lands 'owned' by its several clan components. Face marks usually indicate a person's tribe. But tribes have no elders, ritual leaders or chiefs. In inter-tribal fighting, clans of the same tribe come to the aid of their brethren.

Konkomba, in sum, exemplify a highly decentralised polity organised along typical segmentary lines. They represent about as clear cut a case of anarchy as one can find among African horticulturalists.

Tiv

The Tiv are somewhat similar to the Konkomba, but more structured in their social order. Over a million live in central Nigeria on a rolling plain extending to the banks of the Benue river. Population density is well over a hundred people per square mile. Like the Konkomba, Tiv are also subsistence farmers engaged in grain and yam cultivation. They have few cattle due to the problem of tsetse flies. Their settlements are composed of rather dispersed compounds, each consisting of a ring of huts and connected to other compounds by paths. The segmentary patrilineal system is the fundamental principle of social organisation.

Every Tiv identifies himself with a *tar*, a term like 'country', which refers to a given place associated with a patrilineage. Most men reside in their own home *tar*, but most *tars* have individuals dwelling in them from others. "In time of war, Tiv say, a man must return to his *tar* in order to assist his *ityo* (patrilineage)" (Bohannan, L, 41).

The *ityo* is split into further segments. The ultimate unit is the compound of a family — usually an extended family. Within it the senior male, who is normally also an older man, is responsible for the members and their actions. One who is seen as a continual trouble-maker may be expelled from the compound by the elder. The elder devotes himself to the daily problems of keeping peace and settling quarrels. He must possess the necessary knowledge for peace keeping and, therefore, should know the jural customs, the genealogy and history of his kinsmen, the health and fertility magic, and be in possession of the witchcraft substance, *tsav*. Legitimate power depends on possession of a mystical quality which ensures peace and fertility.

Bohannan lists four relationships in which there is "definite authority" among the Tiv. Three of these are kinship roles: the position of the senior member of the compound mentioned above, the father-son relationship and that of husband and wife. A fourth relationship involving the role of police and judges in the market-place is discussed below.

In addition, there are also men of prestige or influence among the Tiv. These are often elders, but they could be others as well. They possess wealth and demonstrate generosity and astuteness. They were once able to purchase slaves and build up gangs which were used to sell safe conduct to strangers and to rob others. Such individuals were difficult to control. Witchcraft and magic in the hands of the elders were the only effective means of restraining those who were not elders. However, men of prestige who were also elders controlled these supernatural powers too, thus nullifying such attempts to curb them. Therefore travellers seem to have been faced continually with a protection racket.

Elders within a lineage could be called together in assembly to deal with various problems such as occur in connection with witchcraft,[1] magic and curses. These include deaths, sickness, dreams, barrenness, and 'bad luck'. The meeting discusses the matter but has no means to enforce settlements. Good 'judges' are those who get the litigants to concur in a solution which accords with Tiv custom. An elder can only suggest settlement and must work to bring all parties to an agreeable resolution. He is a mediator, not a judge. Witchcraft accusation is very common among the Tiv and it is seen as a cause for innumerable different kinds of events. The elders are invariably reluctant to call a moot to discuss accusations against a man of prestige. In such cases, then, members of a victim's age set, and afterwards members of his own lineage, approach the elders and request an inquest.

For other problems there is no moot or inquest. Rather, the persons involved seek out an elder and ask him to mediate. If a thief has been caught, the victims may go directly to the thief's

---

[1]Witchcraft differs from sorcery. In the latter an individual deliberately carries out specific rituals aimed at injuring another party. In witchcraft is is only *believed* that a person, alleged to be a witch, performs malevolent ritual and non-ritual acts. Of course, such a person also, in fact, holds a position which is feared or resented by the believer in witchcraft.

compound head and demand compensation. In cases of negligence the victim may go directly to the culprit.

The lineage group is not the only source of protection for the individual. Tiv are divided among age sets. Every young man is initiated into a given set and throughout his life he passes or graduates along with his set mates through several grades, each of which is associated with certain communal responsibilities. The age set acts as a peer group mutual aid association, cutting across lineage lines and consolidating individuals from different lineages, but of similar age. Thus a man asks his age set for protection against witches and witchcraft accusations. He may seek assistance for land clearing and other farm work or in financial matters. If one's lineage for any reason withdraws its supernatural protection, a man has his age set as protector. Age sets may assemble to inquire into the health of one of their members.

Among the Tiv the age set system is nowhere near as elaborately developed as among many other African peoples; in fact with the Tiv it is a rather amorphous form of organisation. It appears to be most important to the young adult males as a device for mutual aid and protection. Young men have reason to be wary of the supernatural power and especially the malevolent powers of witchcraft allegedly resting in the hands of the older men. Thus their solidarity at this stage becomes crucial. About age 40, as men pass into eldership roles, the age set function changes to one of protecting the vested interests of eldership against the jealous and resentful. After age 50 the set members constitute a sentimental association: they are no longer competitors.

Between lineage segments there is often feuding and between larger segments fighting can become fierce. But the Tiv also have treaty and pact-making mechanisms. Lineage segments desirous of being able to conduct peaceful trade make treaties with other segments aimed at safe conduct, where otherwise as strangers they would be captured or killed. These treaties "forbid shedding of blood of contracting parties and any act which might lead to it (such as shaving)" (Bohannan, L, 62).

Market pacts secure order in the major local trading centre. This is a market associated with the *tar* which owns the land and controls the market-place. The lineage segment controls the market magic important to securing peace in the market-place, but it also provides market police and judges, all for keeping order. Thus we have within this anarchic polity a circumscribed and restricted area of governmental-style polity. However it should be emphasised that this police power is restricted to the market-place and time and is not generalised outside those boundaries. It suggests that Tiv found traditional techniques of social control inadequate for handling breaches of peace in the market-place and so introduced the police. The Konkomba, too, have markets, each of which is under the control of the clan on whose land the market is located. They, however, do not invoke police. Rather, the market elder has ritual control over a market shrine and he may invoke its supernatural power. Konkomba believe an unconfessed thief would be stung to death by bees which inhabit the trees around the shrine. On confessing his guilt, a thief provides the market elder with a guinea fowl which is sacrificed on the shrine.

The Tiv represent one of the largest and most densely populated of acephalous societies. As with the Konkomba, the segmentary system is of fundamental importance to the political order. This suggests that most of that order is conceived in kinship terms. Yet the Tiv depend upon a number of ancillary systems for maintaining peace. Age sets are important devices for protecting the interests of peer groups. There are treaties and pacts and a rudimentary governmental structure in connection with markets. Underlying the whole system is the power of religious sanctions, which is a power diffused especially in the older members of the community.

Tiv society is one of intergenerational strains: of elders enforcing their authority and younger men resenting it. But when the younger graduate to eldership they too are concerned about maintaining and extending their positions of dominance. As with any age grading system, the individual may find himself in an inferior position, but also has the satisfaction of knowing that eventually, with the passage of time, he too will ultimately graduate to the top of the pile.

The Plateau Tonga

The Plateau Tonga are a matrilineal people living in southern Zambia. They number well over 150,000 with a population density of more than 60 people per square mile. The Tonga keep considerable herds of cattle and are also shifting cultivators, raising corn, millet and sorghum.

The population dwells in tiny villages, from four to eight comprising a neighbourhood cluster. Both because of the poor soil and the shifting cultivation, the location of a village is often changed and there is also some considerable movement of individuals from one location to another in order to establish a new residence.

In addition to residential ties, each Tonga is affiliated to a matrilineal clan, the members of which are scattered throughout the land. These clans have a highly amorphous character: they are not corporate groups; living members never meet as a group and they have no leaders. From the Tonga point of view, however, they are held together by a mystical bond with the ancestral ghosts. Their function seems to be limited to regulating marriage — one cannot marry within the clan — and establishing joking relationships with the members of several other clans. In this way the clan serves as a social control mechanism, since such a relationship prescribes that an individual does not become mad at his joking relative. He engages in an easy-going, light-hearted association and presumably avoids conflict and open expression of hostility. The joking relationship, like that of avoidance, is designed as a technique to promote peace in a relationship which might ordinarily be seen as prone to conflict.

A Tonga also belongs to a matrilineal group within the clan. This is also a dispersed population, but more localised than the clan membership. Thus, a given village will tend to have a high proportion of members of one kin group. The Tonga system should not be seen as a matrilineal counterpart of the patrilineal segmentary system we encountered among the other African peoples. The Tonga are not much interested in genealogical reckoning. There is no internal segmentation or differentiation between the children of one woman within the group and those of another. It is also not at all difficult to become absorbed into a matrilineal group, although, theoretically, membership is based on verifiable descent through the female line. The group also has corporate characteristics. That is, members are jointly responsible for providing bride wealth for their members and for defending their own in feuds. At the same time they share bride wealth received for married daughters and are responsible for taking collective vengeance when one of their number has been murdered, robbed or injured. Inheritance is also governed by matrilineal group membership and there are mutual ritual obligations associated with it as well.

Each Tonga is involved in a complex pattern of relationships and obligations with those in other kin groups beside his own. Thus, one becomes an honorary member of one's father's matrilineal clan. Every household is in some important way a matter of concern not only to the husband's matrilineal group, but also to the matrilineal groups of his wife, his father and his wife's father.

We have also said that each clan is exogamous, but there are other marital regulations which have the effect of requiring that marriages be contracted with a wide variety of different groups, thus cementing alliances with a maximum number.

The neighbourhood in which one lives places on one still further obligations with yet other, unrelated people. Neighbourhoods control land use and exploitation of hunting, fishing and other resources. They obligate residents to a system of mutual aid in a wide variety of activities. Each neighbourhood has its own shrine and constitutes a local 'church'. In connection with this church the entire neighbourhood becomes a congregation for mourning the death of fellow residents, praying for rain and good crops, purifying the land after homicides and celebrating harvests.

Aside from residential and kin ties, the Tonga have an amorphous age grouping system which serves to strengthen intragenerational ties within a neighbourhood. A man may also loan some of his cattle out to others. This establishes new social ties; it also helps minimise the number of stock he might lose from an epidemic or raid. Finally, there are brotherhood pacts which guarantee peaceful movement, especially for trading activity between and among different contracting neighbourhoods.

Villages and neighbourhoods both have headmen and the neighbourhood headman is also priest of the local shrine. Of less significance are leaders of the matrilineal groups. Finally, there are various religious specialists including diviners and those through whom the spirits of the rain speak. A man can compound his importance by acquiring several of these positions. Nevertheless, Tonga leaders are always of *local* importance; there are no leaders or chiefs for all the Tonga.

Positions of prestige and influence are acquired through proving one's reputation as a worthy man. Leadership positions are precarious in the sense that leaders can readily be abandoned by their followers. Headmen act as advisors, mediators and co-ordinators. They might intervene in a dispute, but, like the other mediators we have encountered, they have no authority to enforce their views. At best they might resort to supernatural invocations. Feuds are carried on between clans and between different cult neighbourhoods. They can be brought to an end through agreement to pay damages. The Tonga never act together as a single consolidated unit. No means exist for such a mobilisation. Tonga are apparently not eager to provoke hostilities. They, like other anarchic peoples, "stress the importance of personal restraint in the interests of avoiding any possibility of raising hackles". Colson states that Tonga "attempt to sidestep issues, are reluctant to allow their fellows to drag them into a dispute, and try to vanish from the scene if those in their vicinity seem intent on pursuing a quarrel. Or close supporters, who inevitably will be identified with the combatants attempt to restrain them, taking from their hands any weapons or tools which can be used for injury, applying gentle pressure, and murmuring soothing words about the advisability of cooling the combat for the moment. They do not want to take sides" or draw the wrath of a vengeful person (1974, 39).

The central mechanism of social control in Tonga society is the fact that any given individual is a member of a number of different groups, which in turn are part of a network of further obligations so that any negative action against an individual or group resulting from one set of relationships has its counter restraining effect resulting from affiliation with other groups and individuals. Let us recall that everyone has close ties with his own matrilineal group, that of his father, his mother's father and his father's father. This then establishes a connection with up to four clans. These clan relations are extended through joking relationships and marriage alliances. Further, one belongs to a neighbourhood which draws in still others who are not otherwise part of one's social network. Additionally, one establishes links through cattle loans and brotherhood pacts. By one connection or another a person would ordinarily find that effective restraining measures are built up to cover all the important social relations one might have. The fine mesh of counterbalancing obligations serves to integrate and give order to Tonga society which on the surface at least appears as a society without form. Through such means the Tonga turned 'chiefs', as well as centralised authority and integration, into redundancies.

It is a common misconception that matrilineal societies make women equal to men. But matriliny is not matriarchy. Reckoning descent through females is not rule by females. Of the latter there is no record and for matrilineal societies, such as the Tonga, we find still that men are dominant and have rights and privileges denied the women. It is of course true that in matrilineal societies women often have more leverage than otherwise, since property and status are inherited through affiliation with females. Matriliny, it is sometimes observed, provides a far more unstable kind of social organisation than does patriliny, because inherent in the former is a conflict between inheritance through females, on the one hand, and control of the social order by males, on the other. This conflict often leads to strong pressures towards patriliny, as is testified by African examples, including the Tonga. For the Tonga have deviated from the 'pristine' matrilineal type in

practising virilocal residence[1] and in ascribing no little influence
to the father's kin group.

Two marginal cases: Anuak and Ibo

If the Tiv and Lugbara award certain powers to a man without
making him a king, the Anuak of the southern Sudan perhaps
institute the status of king with its symbolic trappings but stripped
of its powers. These horticultural people live in villages each· of
which has a headman who holds a 'court' and keeps sacred
emblems of the village such as drums and beads. He is approached
by others with signs of respect such as obeisance and the use of a
special vocabulary. Although his house is no better than anyone
else's, the fence posts are decorated with the skulls of animals
killed to provide for the feasts he offers his people. While he has
the trappings of kingship, the headman has in fact little power
and is largely at the mercy of fellow villagers. As long as he can
provide feasts he has good standing and his villagers will see to
it that everyone shows the proper respect to the headman in his
'court'. He is, with the help of other third parties, able to persuade
both the killer of a fellow villager to make compensation and the
victim's kin to accept it.

Anuak, however, do not believe a man should hold the headship
for very long and, definitely, one who can no longer properly feast
his followers deserves no support. He will then find his followers
deserting him. A major faction opposing the headman and no
longer respecting him will arise and install a rival who must be
the son of some previous headman. Such an event leads to fighting
in which the old headman may be deposed. Despite the quarrelling
and intrigue which surrounds the headman office, it does operate
as a unifying force in village affairs, which are otherwise defined by
a segmentary lineage form of organisation similar to that already
discussed. Although different factions may appear in a village, they
are not revolutionary ones: no one seeks to abolish the position of
headman.

In south-eastern Anuak headmen are drawn only from a 'noble'
clan, which apparently comes from outside the Anuak country.
Necklaces, spears, stools and drums are emblems of the office and
there is much struggle, intrigue and fighting to obtain possession of
them. The holder has, as elsewhere in Anuakland, little authority
in his own village, but if he can mobilise an armed force he could

---

[1]Virilocal residence occurs where a newly married couple live in the household of
the husband.

sometimes extend his influence and even gain a usually tenuous control over neighbouring villages.

Thus, among the Anuak, we see the beginnings of a centralisation of authority, based initially upon a ceremonial and symbolic role and expanding in the south-east into a recognisable predatory form of organisation.

Ibo

Another example of rudimentary governmental structure is the Ibo, the second largest ethnic group in southern Nigeria. They presently number some seven million and have traditionally been village-dwelling horticulturalists. Some Ibo, however, have been town dwellers. Marketing and trading are major activities of these people, who are noted for their aggressive business-like activities and their individualism. Throughout Iboland there are at least two different kinds of polity. Thus, some Ibo towns have 'kings' and a governmental structure which is intrusive and not typically Ibo. Over most of Iboland the traditional highly decentralised and acephalous political system has prevailed.

Much of Ibo social life is dependent upon participation within a segmentary lineage structure, the fundamental unit of which is the compound under the supervision of its senior male. Related and neighbouring lineage segments and compounds comprise a village which is ordinarily the maximal unit of social integration and control. Within the village complaints and legal proceedings are undertaken by compound heads, or by groups of mediating third parties each of whom may be called upon to settle a dispute. But such mediators have no power to impose their decisions. Thus, if one is not satisfied by this procedure, one appeals to other institutions. The elders within each village, who form a specific age grade, comprise a deliberative, legislative, judicial and executive body to whom an injured party may appeal. The elders do not act unless they are called upon to do so. They function as a court, deciding guilt or innocence and assessing fines and punishments. Punishments are meted out by the young members of the age grade association. That is, like the Tiv, Ibo have age grades with responsibilities associated with each grade. The members of the younger grade are, among other things, responsible for bringing witnesses and culprits to the village court and for executing punishments decided by the court. Someone found guilty of stealing, for example, may be tied up for days on end without food, or, if he is caught red-handed, he is carried around the village along with what he has stolen and those on the streets curse him, spit on him and ridicule him. There is no power of capital punishment, but a murderer is expected to hang himself if caught.

Aside from this governmental technique, Ibo society has other methods of imposing sanctions. There are associations of titled men which exert considerable influence. These organisations offer various titles which a man may purchase and so acquire prestige. Religious sanctions are imposed by *dibia* associations which are for religious specialists. There are associations for herbalists, for diviners or medicine men; each requires a considerable initiation fee and leads to a member's ordination as a 'priest' within the association. Most important among such individuals are the oracles through whom the gods speak, making predictions, answering questions and, thus, operating as a major force in directing people's behaviour.

Ibo society, to use Bohannan's term, has a multicentric power system: there are several distinct loci of power. Clearly it has a government, but this government is sovereign only over a small population and area and even within it is a diffuse and decentralised arrangement. In addition Ibo society is a stratified society. At the bottom there are slaves, individuals who were captured in warfare and a slightly higher status of cult slaves who are persons who have been dedicated to a deity. Above the slaves are 'pawns', usually young girls, who are pawned to pay for debts. The vast majority of Ibo are freemen, but they are divided between commoners and members of elite groups. Among the latter are senior males of the minor lineages who are empowered to carry wooden club-like objects which are symbols of authority. Others in the upper echelons are the members of the title societies and the various *dibia* societies. Thus, these upper levels of the Ibo world comprise both those who have achieved an elite status by their wealth (title societies) and their learning (*dibia* societies) and those to whom high status has been ascribed as senior lineage males.

New Guinea

Traditional New Guinea is a Tower of Babel of hundreds of different language groups and of thousands of culturally distinct, autonomous villages perched on tropical mountain sides or hidden in secluded valleys. The people raise a variety of tubers and roots and keep pigs. Much energy is devoted to ceremonial and feasting, to carrying on blood feuds and attempting to settle them. The village is a basic social unit. It is composed of several hundred inhabitants, most of whom claim descent through the male line from a common ancestor and so constitute a lineage group.

(There are a few matrilineal groups among New Guineans as well.) Members of such lineage groups make marriages with individuals of other lineages in neighbouring villages and so consolidate alliances with them. Within any given village there are important men of prestige referred to in the literature as 'Big Men'. They acquire followings of dependants — individuals who are in some way in the big man's debt. The Big Man is, in Service's language, a "chief redistributor" of wealth, the 'chief' in control of a redistribution centre.

The lineage system is an important mechanism of social control in New Guinea as in Sub-Saharan Africa. Yet, within this island, there is probably more variety in the system than there is in all of Africa. These New Guinean varieties should not be equated with the typical African segmentary lineage system and they diverge from it in the following ways:

a In much of New Guinea political organisation is a network of inter-village relations, the focus of which is a village. Villages of one ethnic group, situated on the margins of that group's territory, will have the same kind of relationship with those in other ethnic groups as it does with its own;

b New Guinean lineages and clans sometimes do not have a common ancestor or at higher (maximal) levels may not even claim unilineal descent;

c In New Guinea the largest groups which may be considered polities are groups within which no war takes place. But such a unit often does not correspond to other kinds of important maximal social units organised for events such as pig exchanges and initiations. Further, it is sometimes difficult to determine what uniting for war may mean. Thus, among the Siane, there is no war within a phratry. If a clan chooses to go to war outside the phratry, at best it can only be sure that fellow clans will remain neutral. It cannot rely on fellow clans supporting it actively. Clan and lineage in New Guinea are better conceived of as "parameters within which activities are instigated and points of reference fixed to identify individuals and sub groups within publics" (Langness, 1973, 142 ff). There is no automatic alignment of clan, subclan or even lineage behind a man who has been wronged;

d The individual is not seen as the jural representative of lineage or clan. Thus, kin groups are not clearly corporate groups. In these ways New Guinea systems deviate from the African segmentary lineages which are more sharply defined in structure and function and possess a more clearly corporate character.

Lineage groups are important aspects of the New Guinean political system since they carry on blood feuds and settle them.

They are also the groups which, through their adult male members, maintain internal order and peace.

Politically, the most important individuals in a New Guinea community are the Big Men. This too is another contrast with the normal African plan which invests power in the ascribed role of male elder and in the usually achieved roles of religious specialists. The Big Man's leadership accrues from his wealth, his personal charisma, and sometimes from his sheer physical power and size. An example of the latter comes from the Tairora of the Eastern Highlands. They tell a story of Matota who was not only a despot but a fearsome killer as well. Yet he had some reputation as a peacemaker since he had several trading partners and his many wives gave him numerous affines. So he had a wide circle of contacts, acquaintances and presumably friends. On seeing a desirable woman Matota was known merely to motion to the woman's husband and proceed to take her into the bushes. He ordered villagers around with impunity and it was considered that everything in the village belonged to him. He was a symbol of individual initiative, boldness and male machismo — all respected and desirable values among the Tairora. Ultimately he met his own demise in an ambush — the only way such a man could be controlled in this society.

Even in his prime Matota was never despot over more than 2,500 people. His influence and control could not extend far, since not only was it based on a meagre technology of communication and transportation, but it depended as well purely on personal ties and his physical prowess. It could also not lay the basis for creating an hereditary dynasty, since the role of Big Man had to be achieved; it was not inherited. It is likewise a question as to whether Matota himself was conceived of as 'legitimate', or as just a big muscle man. Watson is not sure whether the Tairora case suggests a society which has a leaderless political morality occasionally interrupted by despotism — such as that of Matota. Or does it have a political ideal of the strong leader, but considerable ambivalence about one once he arises? (Watson, *Tairora*, 224 ff.) The case does seem to suggest that where a social system which values individual initiative, male assertiveness and aggressiveness, also lacks control or curbs on such behaviour, despotism must occasionally appear. Under such circumstances there seems no other way to get rid of the despot but to kill him.

Of the Gakuku-Gama, the name for several tribes in the Central Asaro Valley of the Eastern Highlands, Read says that authority is ordinarily achieved and in lieu of any formal political institution "order is maintained largely through self-regulation". There are strong men who have capabilities as warriors and orators and who have proven ability in business, since they own many pigs and contribute considerable amounts to communal feasts which accompany marriages, deaths and other events. Men are admired for their strength and the strong man is a boastful, aggressive person who demonstrates his superiority over others. But to be a strongman also means economic success: one cannot have any debts and must have reciprocated all the gifts made at one's marriage. After this one must acquire sufficient wealth to be able to lend it out to others so as to build up a wide following of debtors. Such persons not only owe the return of the principle, but also a considerable interest as well.

Among the Maring, the Big Man is a physically strong and attractive adult male with a fighting man's temperament and business ingenuity. But Big Men vary according to their ability to communicate with the ancestors. One of the most important positions in Maring society is that of the 'Fight Medicine Man' who has control of 'fight' magic in time of war. Thus religious 'power' is also associated with the Big Men. Similarly among the Wogeo, who inhabit an island off the northeast coast of New Guinea, the leader's influence is derived in large part from his supernatural control of the weather. Wogeo believe he can bring rain or sunshine and hence provoke abundance or famine. Like other Big Men he too provides great feasts and entertainments and so makes others indebted to him. Through his joint religious and economic powers he acquires the right to mediate disputes, although he could do no more than shame individuals into making a settlement (Hogbin, 1979).

Sahlins summarises the Big Man characteristics as personal power, achieved status, an ability to attract a loyal following and to get what he wants done by haranguing his followers; he is not so much a leader as a hero and is able in war, magic, oratory and gardening. One might also add that he is ordinarily a capable mediator. The aim of his economic and political manipulations is to amass goods and distribute them in ceremonies and feasts so as to bring him prestige as a generous man (1963). Perhaps the Big Man is not far removed from Max Stirner's ideal, or the hero in an Ayn Rand novel.

This New Guinean system has close parallels with a *laissez faire* capitalism, but one practised with limited resources. As Sahlins says, it is a highly unstable system: The Big Man reaches a certain stage in his career when he searches for greater and greater renown and is thus driven to press his debtors and other followers for greater production; he in turn delays reciprocities owed to his followers, so that he eventually encourages an 'egalitarian rebellion' which he may try to hold off as long as possible by use of his charismatic and oratorical skills (1963).

The Ifugao

Several peoples in the Philippine Islands have anarchic polities. The Ifugao are probably the best example. They live on the island of Luzon, cultivating mountain gardens and raising chickens and pigs. Their extensive terraces for irrigated rice production are well known. Probably less well known is the fact that this complex system of cultivation is accompanied by a social order in which there is no government, no courts, no judges or constitutional or statutory law.

Ifugao social organisation is extremely simple. As with ourselves, kin relationships are reckoned bilaterally, so that aside from the family household a person identifies with a cognatic group of relatives. While the basic and stable unit is a family centred around its most important member, one is also obligated to go to the defence of any whom one considers within the circle of kinship. Villages hardly exist; rather houses are scattered, sometimes with a cluster of a dozen or so in one place.

Another important aspect of Ifugao social organisation is the division into social strata. At the top is a small group of wealthy men who could at least claim someone in this class, called *kadangyang*, as an ancestor. Admittance to the stratum is achieved by acquiring sufficient wealth to sponsor feasts and become a man of note and influence. The great majority of the Ifugao are either in a middle stratum where a family owns sufficient rice fields to sustain itself, or in a lower class of the poor who have no rice fields.

The *kadangyang* are the leaders of the Ifugao. They are asked to act as go-betweens, that is third party mediators, in disputes. They bring to any negotiations both their own reputation and the power of their own kin group. Particularly favoured are those with a reputation as head hunters. The go-between is employed in a variety of circumstances: in buying and selling operations, borrowing money, marriage proposals, the collection of debts, demands for damages, buying back heads lost in war, ransoming of the kidnapped and making peace. He is responsible to both parties to a dispute and must be impartial, carrying from one group to the other the proper and correct offers and payments. "He wheedles, coaxes, flatters threatens, drives, scolds, insinuates" in trying to bring the parties to an agreement so that he may receive the fee due him. He "has no authority. All that he can do is to act as a peace making go-between. His only power is in his art of persuasion, his tact and his skillful playing on human emotions and motives" (Barton, 87). However, a go-between can compel a defendant to participate in negotiations. If a man tries to run away from, or shows defiance of, an accusation, the go-between seeks him out and with his war knife prominently displayed, therefore forces him to participate. In this aspect we have then a true legal sanction and police authority. We may also understand why an eminent head hunter is preferred for the position.

Besides exacting a fee for his services the go-between also builds his reputation and prestige with every successful settlement so that he will be asked more frequently, acquire more in fees and build his wealth.

Most cases are settled by the assessment of fines. These are determined in part by the nature of the wrong, but there is also a differential scale based on a person's social class. The go-between likewise considers the reputations and positions of the individuals and groups involved. Where fines are to be paid the two parties must first agree on the amount of the payment. Ordinarily the party of the defendant recognises an obligation to pay some indemnity; it mainly tries to reduce the exhorbitant demands of the plaintiff. But, if one side refuses to pay the fines that are assessed, the wronged party may then proceed to attempt to seize property such as gongs, rice wine jars, caraboas, gold beads, children, wives, or rice fields from the culprit.

Sentence of death applies to extreme cases such as murder, sorcery and the refusal to pay a fine for adultery. It is ordinarily carried out by the wronged party. But any 'execution' can have adverse repercussion, since it too may be avenged.

Where an accused denies his guilt he may be asked to undergo the boiling water ordeal. Of course, if he refuses he is considered to be guilty. The go-between acting as an umpire, observes the accused put his hand in a pot of boiling water and remove a stone which has been placed in it. Where two mutually accuse each other their hands are placed side by side and a hot bolo knife is laid on them by the go-between, supposedly only burning the guilty. Wrestling matches and duels are also resorted to. Duels may commence with two opponents throwing eggs, leading to their throwing spears and sometimes to others joining in on the fray.

Feuding is endemic, arising out of the desire to avenge alleged wrongs to one's kin. The taking of the head of an enemy is an important part of the raiding between groups. This prize gives its possessor supernatural power including that of the murdered man. Feuds are sometimes settled by intermarriage and marriage is, in general, a means by which one can extend the network of friendly relations. In addition pacts are made between individuals which guarantee one's safety while in the home district of a pact partner.

Ifugao men and women have fairly equal relationships. This arises in large part from the practice of bilateral kinship. Both man and wife bring to their marriage an equal amount of property and they also work side by side in the fields.

The Land Dayaks

Brief mention might also be made of yet another southeast Asian people: the Land Dayaks of Sarawak in Borneo. They number about 50,000 and are, like the Ifugao, wet rice farmers who also keep pigs and chickens. "The Land Dayaks are anarchists to the extent that no one amongst them is strong enough to force the others to do anything which they do not wish to do. In this classless society there are no true chiefs. Each village has a headman, nowadays confirmed in office by the Government, but he leads only when the people agree to be led. The way he gets his office and the way he uses it ensure that he will not become a dictator" (Geddes, 21). A relative of one who was once a leader is usually favoured to fill the post. A headman is confirmed in his position by general consensus. He should be a man of some wealth, but riches alone do not suffice to make one a great man. A headman, at least, should also be gentle and wise and one who will not seek to rule arbitrarily, forcing his own will on others. Once again we have the man of influence who, if he is tactful, can encourage others to follow his desires.

Any important decisions of the village are decided at a general meeting called by the headman. Here everyone is free to speak and various viewpoints are enunciated with great vigour. A headman observed by Geddes "chose his words carefully, left them unclouded by argument, said them at the right times, and kept them few. Thus, his comments stand out, clear as beacons in the general debate" (Geddes, 22). Since no decision is final unless there is a consensus, occasionally a single stubborn individual can obstruct action which is advocated by everyone else. "In such a case the unanimity which closes the meeting is an agreement to do nothing" (Geddess, 22). Ordinarily agreement is reached in part because public opinion is a strong force which only the most thick-skinned can ignore.

In most villages there are one or two older men who know a sufficient amount about the genealogies of their neighbours to settle any of the rare disputes which do arise concerning land. The Land Dayaks also have quasi-specialist religious leaders. Some of these lead ceremonies connected with the veneration of ancestors and others are shamans who tend to concentrate on the diagnosis and cure of illnesses, most of which are believed to be caused by demons.

Like the other groups discussed in this essay, there is no overall political integration of the Dayak society. Each village is an autonomous and independent entity which may have either friendly or hostile relations with its neighbours.

South American Indians
The sub-tropical and tropical regions of South America were home to a multitude of differing cultural groups. Most of them were small in population with no political integration beyond a local level. Some were clearly anarchic; others were not.

Dole points to several examples of South American forest Indians wherein a hereditary chieftainship was extremely powerful. A Sherente headman was obeyed when he ordered several other men to kill a man who had repeatedly abandoned his wife. Apinaye headmen ordered the execution of alleged sorcerers. A Shavante headman held five men to be dangerous to communal well-being and had them executed. The Cashinahua headman visited every family in his village each day and gave out orders for the day's activities. His permission was also required before a marriage could be contracted.

Dole suggests that perhaps many of the known anarchic tribes in South America were once much less so and considers in some detail the case of the Kirikuru, a small group of about 145 persons who live in central Brazil.

They have 'headmen' who have no authority or power, although they once had more before recent demographic and social disturbances. Disease has reduced the population of many groups to the point where they can no longer function as self-sufficient and separate entities. Consequently various remnant groups consolidate. Thus among the Kirikuru there are people from at least four different 'tribes'. Headmanship was normally a kind of hereditary office through the male line, but a man often dies before his eldest son matures so that one from another family is therefore appointed. This man himself may be from a family which had provided headmen in another tribe. Thus leadership is distributed among various families producing claims to succession in several patrilines so that the position becomes weakened. Dole argues that the strength of headmanship is tied to lineality because it provides a standardised and exclusive channel for the exercise and transmission of authority. Where, as with the Kirikuru, this disappears, the authority of the headman is undermined.

In lieu of any chiefly power Kirikuru rely upon a number of diffuse sanctions. There is gossip, complaining, and ostracism. Alleged sorcerers and witches are killed; guilt in connection with a crime or evil is determined by divination. Any woman who looks on the secret flutes of the tribe is punished by gang rape.

Lowie presents examples of the chiefly role among other South American tribes. The Caraja chief is wholly dependent on his villagers' goodwill. If they are dissatisfied with him they will only abandon him. The Tapuya chief was highly respected when he was leading his warriors, but at home he was not so honoured. The modern Taulipang "headman has very little to say until hostilities break out with another group" (Lowie, 1949, 341). The Jivaro likewise emphasise chieftainship only in time of war. Indeed, they have no term for chief in their vocabulary and their war leaders are only of a temporary kind. Actually over the long term a shaman may be the most influential man in a Jivaro community. He is a curer, a maker of love potions, a diviner of enemy activity and interpreter of omens of defeat or victory in war. At the same time he may also be the war leader.

The more anarchic of the South American polities are made up of groups of kinsmen so that social relationships are kinship relationships. The chiefly role as Lowie sees it, entails acting as peacemaker, representing the group in foreign relations, welcoming visitors, directing economic activities and indulging in admonishing harangues (Lowie, 1949, 343).

Pierre Clastres has focussed on the more anarchic tribes in South America. He asks why the chief should have no power. He recognises the chief's importance as a peacemaker and mediator, but argues that these functions should not be confused with the nature of chieftainship. To explain this nature we must turn to the relationship of the chiefly role to reciprocity. The chief is involved in an exchange entailing women, words and wealth. Most of these Indians practise polygyny. The chief is always the man with the most wives; often the only polygynist in the group. At the same time the chief is expected to enthral the group with his oratory — no speech, no chief. He must sponsor feasts, support the community in hard times and always demonstrate his magnanimity and generosity. Through these mechanisms the chief continually strives to validate and revalidate his position. But such demonstrations are not, as one might think, proper reciprocations to the community for the excess of wives or the position the chief has. Women are of such 'consummate' value that all the words and all the gifts provided by the chief are insufficient to qualify the situation as a reciprocal, that is, equal exchange. As such the chief in his position defies reciprocity, that basic law of social relations. Such an asymmetrical relationship is identified with power and that in turn with nature. In opposition to them stand reciprocity,[1] society and culture. People in archaic societies, realising this conflict and the contradiction of the fundamental social law, see power as enjoying a privileged position. It is therefore dangerous and in need of restraint; in fact 'power' should be made 'impotent'. The final synthesis in this dialectic is paradoxical. The chief's most unreciprocal acquisition of multiple wives puts him in a condition of perpetual indebtedness to his people, so that he must become their servant.

Clastres' argument is both plausible and logical. Yet reason and logic alone are clearly insufficient grounds for accepting a theory. For the more empirically-minded, Clastres' explanation, like other structuralist explanations, seems strangely detached from the solid earth. The use of hard evidence to demonstrate the theory is lacking. We are given no idea of what the individuals involved may think. But then the structuralists argue that these things are superficial appearances, not the world in reality, the deep, underlying structure. Structuralism, like Freudianism, Jungianism and, to a lesser extent, Marxism, suffers from the problem of testability. A scientific hypothesis or theory should be so constructed that it is falsifiable. It should be subject to empirical test such that different investigators should be able to analyse the same phenomenon and validate the hypothesis by independently coming to the same conclusions. Strangely enough both Levi-Strauss and Clastres have investigated the chiefly role in South America according to structuralist principles, but have apparently reached different conclusions about it. In contrast to Clastres, Levi-Strauss offers the usual conservative explanation that a true reciprocal relationship is involved. (Levi-Strauss, 309). Clastres correctly expresses concern about the ethnocentrism inherent in much political anthropology and in cultural evolutionary doctrine. He also calls our attention to the opposition and tension between reciprocity and leadership.

---

[1]Such emphasis upon reciprocity perhaps implicitly over-emphasises the altruism involved, neglecting the fact that many people do not give in the 'spirit' of reciprocity so much as out of a fear of reprisal if they do not give (Colson, 1974, 48).

Bibliographic note
The following are the main sources used for African peoples:
Lugbara, Middleton; Konkomba, Tait; Tiv, Laura and Paul
Bohannan; Tonga, Colson; Anuak, Evans-Pritchard; Ibo, Green
and Uchendu. The New Guinea materials are from Berndt and
Lawrence, Hogbin, Langness, Pospisil, Read, Sahlins, and Watson.
The Ifuago are based on Barton and the Dayak on Geddes. South
American Indians are from Clastres, Dole, Lowie, and Steward
and Faron.

V

Anarchist Herders

Our third kind of society concerns those people who specialise in the rearing of livestock. This does not include those who, as in our society, specialise in producing livestock for sale in a market, but only those who rely on domesticated animals as their chief mode of subsistence. Indeed, marketing such animals is viewed by some pastoral people as almost sacrilegious.

Pastoralism possibly originates as a speciality in agricultural village life. Early farmers – five or six thousand years ago in the Near East – may have initially sent their livestock out of the village each day, or for longer periods, to graze under the direction of herdsmen. In the course of time the latter separated from the village so that they commenced keeping their own animals, utilising as grazing grounds the marginal lands which were not good for agriculture. Eventually the pastoral specialty spread through central Asia and large parts of Africa outside the rain forest zone. Wherever it developed it was readily adapted to local conditions, so that several types of pastoralism survive to this day.

Pastoral peoples rely upon a few varieties of livestock. In all cases their animals are grazers and browsers which are on the move cropping grasses and shrubs. These animals include: equids (donkey and horse), camelids (camels and llamas), bovids (cattle, yaks and buffalo), ovids (sheep and goats) and cervids (reindeer). Thus pastoralists may be divided as:

1   Llama herders in highland regions of western South America
2   Reindeer herders of Arctic and Sub Arctic Eurasia.
3   Central Asiatic herders of mixed stock including, sheep, goats, horses, cattle and sometimes camels and yaks. For the Central Asians sheep and goats are the cornerstone of the economy, except in Tibet where yaks are of most crucial importance.

4 Middle Eastern herders of sheep, goats and camels, with hroses and donkeys in aminor role. For some, camels are paramount; others, as in eastern Turkey and Iran, have camels, but sheep and goats are more important.
5 Herders of the African savannah grasslands depend on cattle, but
sheep and goats are also kept and in a few cases so are donkeys and horses.

Except among reindeer and llama herders, livestock is mainly the provider of milk and other dairy products. Indeed, aside from the donkey and llama, all the animals used by herders are milked in at least one place or another. The herds contribute to the economy in other ways as well. The larger animals are important as means of transportation – for movement of both baggage and person; they provide the meat that is consumed at all festive and cere monial occasions. Their hair, wool and hides are used for making clothing, shelters, containers, harness and many other things. Even their urine and manure is important among some pastoralists.

Most pastoralists engage in activities other than herding for a livelihood. Nearly all indulge in a somewhat indifferent cultivation, providing chiefly grain. Some are occasional fishermen, while hunting and gathering are of minor importance. One of the distinguishing features of pastoralists, especially in the Middle East and to a lesser extent in Central Asia and arctic Eurasia, is the symbiotic tie to a sedentary cultivating and town-dwellling population. The close interaction with these peoples often affords an opportunity to acquire wealth by raiding, warfare and extortion. In the latter case there is a kind of protection racket, wherein sedentary villagers and townsmen pay tribute to the pastoral tribe to avoid being raided. Furthermore, most pastoralists depend upon townsmen for much of their manufactured goods and other supplies and on peasant villagers for agricultural products. Many pastoral systems are then, as Kroeber called them, 'part cultures', not fully self-sufficient entities either in terms of material productivity, or in terms of the ideological and spiritual aspects of life.

Nearly all pastoral peoples are in part at least nomadic. There are those who live their entire lives in dwellings which are readily transportable and they move in a seasonal round over a tribal territory following their grazing herds. Others may spend part of the year in nomad encampments and part in fixed village houses, while some such as the Nuer, to be considered below, send their herds off with all the young people as herders during the extended dry season while the elders remain at home in the village.

The tribal form of social organisation described in the previous chapter prevails among herders. The chief exception is among some of the reindeer keepers of northern Eurasia, especially the Samek who have essentially a band type organisation like that of hunter-gatherers. The tribal structure entails a segmentary patrilineal kind of organisation. But in many cases this has evolved into a kind of incipient state structure with distinct social classes and a military organisation which undertakes true warfare.

Pastoralism ordinarily supports relatively large and dense populations and in some cases, for example, Genghis Khan's Mongols, has allowed for the creation of extensive, though ephemeral, empire states. In part because of the marginal nature of their enterprise and because they are motivated to increase herd size and so expand grazing areas, pastoralists, especially in southwest Asia and Africa, have acquired reputations as warriors and predators.

The Nuer

There are some herders who have perpetuated a segmentary patrilineal 'tribal' system without government and as such exemplify the practice of anarchy. Clearly the most famous example is the Nuer, an Nilotic people presently numbering probably 400,000, who reside in the swampy Sudd area of the White Nile and its vicinity in the southern part of the Republic of Sudan.

We have encountered the segmentary lineage system several times before and the Nuer system is basically no different from that of the Lugbara or Konkomba. There are local villages which are identified with lineage segments and inhabited largely by members of that segment, but there are outsiders in a village as well. In addition, members of the lineage associated with a given village will be found dwelling in other villages. Members of the clan segments are likewise dispersed. Village territories identified with given lineages combine to form larger territorial units associated with yet larger segments (subclans and clans), until one encompasses a tribal domain which is inhabited by members of the tribe.

A tribe may have between 5-45,000 people. Each is economically self-sufficient, having all its own pastures, water supply and fishing places. Within the tribe disputes between members ought to be settled by mediation and members ought to unite against other tribes and foreigners. If a Nuer leaves his own tribal domain and settles in another he thereby changes his tribal affiliation and becomes a member of the tribe within whose territory he now lives. This is because hostilities between tribes are endemic and there is no obligation to mediate. On the other hand, one may move from one lineage territory within the same tribal domain to another without changing one's lineage affiliation.

In addition to the lineage structure, Nuer have age grades which cut across lineage affiliations and tribal membership, uniting individuals of the same sex and approximate age. It is a much weaker structure than may be found among many other Africans, including the Tiv, and is largely a device for noting the rites of passage between childhood, youth, adulthood. Women also have a parallel organisation to that of the men. Age grades have no political function and aparently do not even act as mutual aid associations.

The feud between segments of the same complementary level of the system is the primary political mechanism among the Nuer. Thus, if a man kills a member of a different subclan, a feud situation would exist between the subclans of the aggressor and his victim. However, the feud in fact will involve only close kinsmen on both sides. the more inclusive the segments become – that is, the higher one goes among groups in the levels of segmentation – the more difficult it becomes to settle a dispute, so that conflicts between members of primary or secondary tribal sections often lead to intertribal fights (see diagram under discussion of Lugbara above).

Disputes, including feuds, are regulated and usually ultimately settled through the mediation of a man known as the leopard skin chief. As Evans-Pritchard has noted, the title 'chief' is misleading since he has no true chiefly powers but is rather a ritual specialist who belongs to one of a limited number of lineages. The leopard skin chief is much like the Lugbara rainmaker. Someone who commits a murder first goes to the chief whose residence is a sanctuary. The chief cuts the arm of the murderer as a mark of Cain. He may then act as a mediator between the kin of the killed and of the killer. He insures that the latter are willing to pay blood money so as to avoid feuding and then persuades the other group to accept compensation. The leopard skin chief collects the blood money in the form of cattle, from 40-50 animals, and takes them to the dead man's home. The chief does not act as judge, although he may be very insistent and even threaten to curse the dead man's kin if they do not accept compensation. But threats are invariably made, because that group must preserve its honour and so appear reluctant to accept. What is of paramount importance is the "moral obligation to settle the affair by the acceptance of a traditional payment and the wish, on both sides, to avoid for the time being at any rate, further hostilities" (Evans-Pritchard, 1961, 292).

"The leopard skin chief does not rule and judge, but [is a] mediator through whom communities desirous of ending open hostilities can conclude an active state of feud" (Evans-Pritchard, 1961, 293). He may also mediate in disputes concerning ownership of cattle. In any case all the leopard skin chief can do is ask the parties to discuss a conflict and only if both sides are agreeable to mediation can the matter be settled. The ultimate power of the leopard skin chief, as with that of the Lugbara rainmaker, is to curse those who will not agree to a suggested settlement. This is indeed the nearest the Nuer come to any governmental structure and for someone who firmly believes in the power of the curse it possesses, therefore, a similar authority and force to a policemen in our society ordering someone off to jail at the point of his pistol. On the other hand, the curse, unlike the policeman's pistol, is not a weapon legitimately confined to the leopard skin chief alone, for others as well have the power to invoke the supernatural, though it may not be as potent a force. Furthermore, the power of the chief is apparently only legitimate within the narrow limits of accepting the results of mediation. Its authority does not extend to other areas of social control.

The leopard skin chief incidentally decides appropriate compensations in accord with well-established Nuer custom, but as Evans-Pritchard makes clear, this does not make a legal system "for there is no constituted and impartial authority who decides on the rights and wrongs of a dispute and there is no external power to enforce such a decision were it given" (1961, 293).

Aside from the leopard skin chiefs, the most important men among the Nuer are the local heads of extended families. These are older men, but above all they are men rich in the number of cattle and men who have the kind of personality respected by all Nuer. They also belong to what Evans-Pritchard refers to as aristocratic clans. Such groups are those which predominate within a given tribe. The term 'aristocratic' seems inappropriate since such a clan has prestige, but no special privilege and does not even have prestige outside of its own tribe. These influential individuals lack any clearcut status. "Every Nuer . . . considers himself as good as his neighbour, and families and joint families, whilst co-ordinating their activities with those of their fellow villagers, regulate their affairs as they please. Even in raids there is very little organisation and leadership is restricted to the sphere of fighting and is neither institutionalised nor permanent" (Evans-Pritchard, 1961, 294).

The Nuer do have several different kinds of ritual specialists: The Man of the Cattle, totemic specialists, rainmakers, fetish owners, magicians, diviners. Yet none has any political status or function, except that some do become prominent and are able to scare others by their alleged supernatural powers.

As with the Lugbara, 'prophets' appeared as an additional political force among the Nuer in the late 19th century, probably provoked by the Mahdist phenomenon in the Sudan. The early prophets seem to have been ritual specialists — healers and shamans — and later to have acquired roles as mediators of disputes within their own districts. Some prophets were able to imbue a sense of tribal unity, with themselves as symbols of that unity, by inciting the several factions of their tribe to united action in war against some enemy. It was the prophets who organised the tribes to which they belonged to fight both Arab and European incursions. But they never integrated any group larger than their own tribe and even these efforts were short-lived.

Egalitarianism and cattle pastoralism

Harold K Schneider argues the thesis that there is a significant relationship between egalitarianism and dependence upon cattle pastoralism. Focussing on East Africa, he finds that those societies which have a high ratio of cattle to humans (more than one per person) are egalitarian and stateless, with social systems which are either primarily organised around the segmentary lineage concept or around age grading. Hierarchy and the state tend to appear more commonly amongst people with fewer cattle. He believes reliance upon cattle production by its nature inhibits the growth of hierarchical organisation. Cattle herds provide a highly mobile source of wealth which can grow rapidly and can also as rapidly be wiped out. Where cattle rearing is the primary focus of the economy and involves the participation of all it is difficult to monopolise the main source of wealth or bring it under the control of the few. "It is difficult . . . to centralise cows" (Schneider, 219).

In addition, Schneider emphasises the widespread importance of stock associations in which cattle are lent out to other men. Consequently every man becomes involved in a network of relations in which each is a lender and a borrower of cattle. This has the manifest function of minimising losses from raids and disease. It builds goodwill with others, lessens pressures on grazing land and spreads the burden of work. At the same time it helps to disguise one's own wealth. But more importantly, these stock associations lend reinforcement to the hierarchy-inhibiting features of cattle raising, by engaging each man in a multiplicity of equal and mutual bonds with others. Egalitarian systems are such because they provide "multiple opportunities for acquiring new wealth, so that men of substance, big men as opposed to chiefs, were seldom able to translate wealth into power since those whom they sought to dominate had resources, derived from multiple opportunities and wide ranging systems of stock association credit in an atmosphere of rapid capital formation, which allowed them to escape submission" (Schneider, 210). Egalitarianism always "rests upon an economic base which is such that by its nature (and sometimes perhaps by legal arrangement) it cannot be monopolised" (Schneider, 219).

It is interesting that Schneider places considerable emphasis upon stock associations (and possibly correctly), but the Nuer which we have discussed above are invariably taken as *the* example of the typical cattle pastoralist, egalitarian society and they do not seem to depend to any extent on this mechanism. They do have an institution called *math* or 'best friend' in which two men formally establish a bond of friendship by exchanging or loaning cattle (Howell, 198). I have not found *math* described in any published source in any detail. Either it is not of much importance to the Nuer or, as may very well be the case, Evans-Pritchard and others who have studied the Nuer never recognised its significance.

In his book Schneider does not address the question of why pastoral peoples outside of East Africa tend more often to have hierarchical systems and proto-states, if not full blown states. Central Asian stockmen from Soviet Turkestan to Mongolia not only depended upon large herds of sheep, but also on herds of cattle and horses as well. They also organised some very substantial states and hierarchical systems. Arab Bedawin and Iranian pastoralists also seem much more oriented to systems far less egalitarian than East African herders. Yet one important difference between Asiatic and African pastoralists is that the former have always dwelt in close proximity to large states (China, Iran and the Indian states). Perhaps, then, the evolution of hierarchical structures amongst the Asiatic peoples is a response to this circumstance. Notables among the pastoralists acted as intermediaries with the giant states and were central figures in the very important trade activity between China and the West through such channels, then, pastoral notables were able to enhance their power and create states.

Schneider also does not consider the many African cultivators, many of whom have few livestock of any kind, who have egalitarian, anarchic social orders (eg, Konkomba, Tiv, etc). One is led to wonder, therefore, whether the basis for egalitarian and acephalous systems is not so much dependence upon a highly mobile and reproductive form of wealth (cattle) as it is dependence upon a cultural pattern which induces a maximal dispersal of counterbalancing social bonds, and creates an atmosphere in which monopoly is impossible. Monopolies *can* be created with cattle and monopolies may be made impossible with other forms of wealth. One might compare the Mongol herders on the one hand with the Konkomba cultivators on the other.

The Samek or Lapps

Reindeer herding in the European sub-Arctic is in sharp contrast to the lanky Nuer pasturing his cattle in the torrid southern Sudan. Yet these peoples share not only pastoral life, but an individualistic world view and anarchic social structure as well. While the Samek have generally shown a remarkable tenacity in maintaining their unique culture in the face of centuries of intimate contact with Europeans, they have nevertheless modified their political and religious systems as a consequence of this contact. For 300 or more years it can be said that the Samek have been subject to the rule of one or the other of the Scandinavian or Russian states and they have likewise been subject to either Lutheran or Orthodox Christian churches. It is therefore somewhat difficult to reconstruct the more 'pristine', pre-contact social order of the Samek.

For one thing it is obvious that the Samek never had any overall political integration. They were a people divided among many small herding bands, each of which was an independent and autonomous entity. The band is still important among the Samek. Despite the fact that the Samek are a pastoral people, this basic social unit, the band, is similar to that which characterises most hunting-gathering people. Thus the Samek band consists of a few dozen people, most of whom are related to one another. This relationship is bilateral; it may be either through the father or the mother. Indeed, Samek kinship, like that of the Inuits and of Europeans, is quite non-lineal. Members of the band have use rights to a certain territory; thus, it could be said that the territory is the collective property of the group. Band members have the exclusive right to hunt and fish in the area and of paramount importance is the right to pasture their reindeer.

Band membership has a rather fluid character in that it is perfectly possible for one to withdraw from a group and seek membership in another. It seems that at one time the band was an exogamous group and thus engaged in the cementing of alliances with other similar groups through the exchange of women as wives.

Internal affairs are managed by what some writers have called a council. Since this body included in its membership the heads of every family, the term 'council' is in fact somewhat misleading in its connotation of formal organisation and delegation of power. Group decisions are actually the collective responsibility of the adult male population as a whole — a common feature of the other anarchic polities which we have encountered.

There is in addition a band leader. This is a position for life and is often hereditary, passing to the eldest son. But sometimes the leader might be selected by the group. It is even possible for a man to marry into a situation where he can eventually become leader because the present one is his father-in-law, who has no sons to succeed him. Ordinarily a leader should be wealthier than any of his colleagues. Band leaders are essentially chief herdsmen of the group in that their authority over other individuals encompasses their relationship to the reindeer herds. The band leader is then co-ordinator of the group's major economic activity. "It is he who determines which kin groups within the band shall furnish personnel for a herding expedition. It is he who sets migration dates, accepts or rejects an applicant for band membership, and directs herd movements. It is he who gives some continuity and stability to the loosely organised Lapp band since his successor is usually chosen from among his sons or sons-in-law." Outside the sphere of herd management the role of the leader "is ambiguous and he is frequently overruled in group decisions" (Pehrson, 1077).

'Master of the band' is the literal translation of the Samek title and 'mistress of the band' is the equivalent term for the wife or mother of the band leader. She has a considerable amount of influence within the group. Indeed, Samek society like that of the Inuit, Ifugao or Dayak awards a much more equal position to women in general. Women inherit equally with men; they could transmit property the same as men; they participate fully in the economic activities of the group and male leadership of the band itself could be transmitted through a woman.

Another source of power in the Samek community in pre-Christian times was the shaman. Details of Samek shamanism are not well known, but it seems safe to say that such individuals, being the most skilled in communicating with the supernatural, in curing illness and in divining future events, were ones to be listened to and respected. It is hard to believe that they did not sometimes seek to use their powers to enhance their own personal positions within a neighbourhood.

Modern times have been accompanied by the expansion of individual property (enlargement of herds, acquisition of modern technology such as snowmobiles, etc) and this has tended to increase the individualism within Samek society. At the same time the governments of Sweden, Norway, Finland and the Soviet Union have instituted formalised techniques to foster more direct control over Samek social affairs.

Bibliographic note:
The chief source for the Nuer is Evans-Pritchard. Other African pastoralists with acephalous political systems, some of which approach the anarchy of the Nuer are the Barabaig (see Klima); Dinka (see Lienhardt); Jie (Gulliver); Karamojong (Dyson Hudson); Turkana (Gulliver). For the Samek see Pehrson and Vorren and Manker.

VI

Anarchy in Agricultural Societies

Almost by definition one would not expect examples of anarchic polities among agricultural peoples. Among the reasons for this is the fact that agriculture entails permanent cultivation of large tracts of land so there is an incentive to accumulate this important resource as property. Further, agriculture from its inception was, and still today is, widely associated with irrigation. Due to the complex problems of water distribution, irrigation can easily lend itself to bureaucratization or at least it has often done so. Consequently, it is easy for a stratified and politically centralized society to arise within the context of agriculture. Agricultural peoples include those who share a peasant way of life, which is followed today probably by a good minority of humankind. In addition, modern industrial societies fall into this category as well, so that altogether over 90% of the world's population is presently encompassed in this type.

Although no pristine examples of anarchy seem to be traditionally practiced by any agricultural people, there are interesting cases of highly decentralised confederations which border on anarchy and whose governmental institutions are of the most ambiguous kind.

Consider ancient Iceland. This bleak island was settled in 864 by Norsemen, no small number of whom moved because they were outlawed in Norway or were dissatisfied with conditions there. One must remember that nearly all the settlement of Iceland occurred before Norway developed any system of a unified or centralised state and monarchy. Settlers did bring with them the Germanic-Norse conception of 'law', an important ingredient of which was the notion of the assembly of free adult males to legislate and pass sentence upon criminals, all by a system of consensus.

The new settlers in Iceland introduced the stratified social

system of Scandinavia. There were the freemen who laid claim
to homesteads in the new land and there were hired hands or
bondsmen (thralls). From the freemen were drawn 36 chiefs
(*godhis*) who, with their families, constituted the aristocracy.
Each chief was the senior man in his given area, which in the
early period would have included barely 1,000 inhabitants. He
protected those dwelling in his territory and helped the freemen
in securing their rights. He was the main decision-maker to whom
people deferred; he also attempted to mediate disputes and punish
culprits. It might be said that his sword was feared not necessarily
because it was wielded by the most able fighter, but because there
was attached to it an aura of legitimate authority. But while there
was then a vague legal sanction associated with the *godhi*, he was
basically a man of influence who was successful in imposing his
will to the extent that he could convince his followers to accept
him as their first among equals. When the community withdrew
its goodwill the chief was powerless. He had no police force to
support him, only the public opinion which he tried to rally to
his support. Thus a good chief was one respected and admired
by his followers so that they supported him. A bad chief would
find his will frustrated, his following declining and ultimately his
own gory demise. Individual freemen who disliked their chief might
renounce their allegiance to him and accept another. Because of
this, a given chiefdom was not characterised by a true notion of
territorial sovereignty, since a given territory identified with one
chief might actually be dotted with farms whose owners adhered
to another.

From very early times, in Iceland all the habitable lands in the
island were occupied and claimed as homesteads, the owners of
which were associated with one chief or another. The Icelandic
hinterland, a land dominated by icefields and live volcanoes, was
a refuge for those who rejected the system or who were outlawed
by the rest of society.

The local political unit then was a chiefdom which lacked a
clean cut sovereign territory. There was no real executive power
and diffuse sanctions were the primary means of social control.
A chiefdom was not a sovereign state, but was rather a voluntary
contractual relationship between chief and freeman which could be
broken at will by a freeman.

Beyond this local chiefdom, the only form of political integration
in early Iceland centred around the 'Things'. These were
voluntary judiciary assemblies of freemen led by the chiefs
"where mutual problems were discussed according to orderly
traditional procedures" (Thompson, 165). There were regional

Things and one Althing for the whole island. The latter met annually and here participants were reminded of the customary 'law'; they also legislated new regulations and performed as a court. But none of the Things were truly governmental institutions since they had no power to enlist a military force, nor had they any means, aside from urging diffuse sanctions, to enforce what was decided. The most common punishments entailed outlawry (banishment from civilised society for a set number of years) and confiscation of a man's property. The enforcement of outlawry depended entirely on the public's willingness to see that the man was banished. And as the Sagas tell us, a banished man invariably found supporters who would aid him, so that banishment was by no means the harsh punishment one might imagine in a place like Iceland. Furthermore it seems from the Sagas that implementation of banishment was left up to those who belonged to the wronged party; other individuals were at best indifferent regarding enforcement (cf. *Saga of Gisli, Saga of Grettir the Strong*).

In the other form of punishment — the confiscation of property — it was necessary for a number of men from the Thing to take it upon themselves as a collective whole to visit the homestead of the condemned and declare the property confiscated. The men assuming this responsibility appear also to have been the aggrieved individuals and their friends. If no such group took up this task the judgement of the Thing remained unenforced. When there was an attempt to confiscate property it frequently led to feuding and acts of vengeance. A chief who was found guilty of an offence by the Thing might defy the sentence and this too usually resulted in blood feud.

Icelandic Things had no executive officer. The Althing, for example, appointed a man for a three year term as 'lawman' whose responsibility it was to recite one third of the law each year and also to act as a moderator at the Althing meeting, a position similar to that of a moderator of a New England town meeting — as a 'non-partisan' who merely calls upon various individuals who wish to speak.

Social order in ancient Iceland rested upon the voluntary contractual agreement with a *godhi* and upon judgements of an assembly of all adult freemen in which enforcement depended upon voluntary collective or diffuse sanctions. But one might also resort to blood feud and sorcery to obtain justice and order. Even if the Althing passed judgement on a man for murder, the honour of the murdered man's kinsmen required revenge and thus feuds seem to have been very common and only stopped when cooler heads sought to intervene and begin a process which would bring the issue to a Thing for settlement. Sometimes this settlement was cause for renewed bloodshed.

A man also defended his honour and pride by duelling, the consequences of which likewise provoked feuding. Both men and women could obtain a reputation as powerful magicians so that their manipulation of supernatural forces was greatly feared.

While there were men who obtained reputations as mediators of disputes in Iceland (such as Njall in *The Burnt Njall*) the institutionalisation of mediation was primarily in the Thing.

Laura Thompson described the ancient Icelandic commonwealth as ". . . in actuality not one state but rather a confederation of independent, politically equal godord associations" (Thompson, 163). Of course it must be remembered that one of the reasons for this situation was that the several chiefs were jealous of their own realms of power and influence and so attempted to curtail centralisation of authority. However the struggle between chiefs even eventually led to the supremacy of fewer and fewer of them. Finally one chief became dominant and made Iceland a Norwegian dependancy. Iceland was thus being rapidly divested of its old decentralist, headless and anarchic characteristics — characteristics which, to contemporary Europeans, were rather incredible 'barbarisms'.

Imazighen or Berbers

Throughout the Middle East there are several different ethnic groups which have been referred to as 'inhabiting lands of insolence' because they live in defiance of centralised government authority. They are 'tribally' organised, with patrilineages and highly decentralised, acephalous polities. Imazighen who dwell in northern Algeria and in the Moroccan highlands probably demonstrate the more anarchic of these peoples. A most appropriate example is the so-called 'Kabyle' — Imazighen farmers of northern Algeria and a group noted with favour by Kropotkin.

The fundamental social unit in Kabyle society is the family household. Several adjacent households comprise a neighbourhood within a village and this is equivalent to a common patrilineage, although it may include persons who are not true kinsmen. The patrilineage, in turn, is a constituent of a clan. Ordinarily there are two clans in a village each identified with a *sof* or moiety — that is, one particular half of the village. Villages are independent entities. From ten to 20 comprise a tribe, but this has no effective function, being at best a voluntary association or alliance called into being on rare occasions for mutual defence. About a dozen tribes are to be found in Kabylia.

Each lineage in a village has a chief spokesperson who participates in a village council which deliberates on all matters of communal importance: legislating, mediating and judging. The council is expected to defend the honour of the community and to see to it that its decisions are carried out. Here, as in other cases encountered in this survey, we may note the weakness of true governmental features since there are no specific policemen. Rather the council usually seeks to mediate between disputants trying to find some basis for compromise and exhorting them to reach an agreement. Once again the aim seems to be not so much to determine guilt as to re-establish group harmony. The council is, in fact, the voice of public opinion and communal sanctions, since it is composed of representatives of each kin group, also because it acts only when agreement is unanimous, that is, by consensus. The two primary forms of punishment which may be imposed by this body are banishment from the village and ostracism. The council, as has been said, is essentially the voice of village public opinion and if it chooses to ostracise a fellow villager, all others tend to fall in line to enforce the punishment which is seen as a symbolic putting to death. Similar diffuse and collective sanctions operate in banishing a member.

The collective oath is resorted to as a final resort, when every other method of settlement has failed. This entails the members of a group jointly swearing to the truth of their claims on pain of the wrath of God if perjury is committed. Thus a refusal to swear is an admission of guilt.

Aside from the council of the whole village, the males of a lineage on occasion may meet as a body, but more important is the council of the clan which controls the time of commencement of various seasonal activities such as the beginning of ploughing, harvesting and other communal labour, as well as the religious festivals. Throughout, councils always operate on the basis of a well-known collection of customary regulations peculiar to the village. These delineate the recognised 'crimes' and their appropriate punishments. In addition councils are guided by a Kabyle code of honour.

Bourdieu calls the Kabyle system a 'gentilitial democracy' since it is a group of kinsmen who administer their lives through an assembly of all the 'fathers' in the village. Yet it seems to lack some essential attributes of democracy. First, the majority does not rule: consensus is the basis for decision-making. Secondly, ideally at least, power is so decentralised that every kin group in the community is represented. Delegation of authority, a characteristic of democracy, can hardly be said to exist. Thirdly, enforcement of decisions is not through policemen and the council is not a judicial body so much as it is a mediatory one. Ultimate power rests in the expression of the diffuse sanctions of the community. Finally, the social intercourse is more in the nature of a relationship between kinsmen than it is a political affair. In these respects then we have an institution which seems more anarchic than it is democratic.

Among Moroccan Imazighén a patri lineage system along with the respective councils is also characteristic. Yet the structure at the higher levels of integration is more distinct and powerful, such that tribal councils are clearly in evidence as governing bodies. A tribal council consists of the patriarchs from each of the several clans which make up the tribe. These patriarchs often constitute a kind of nobility from which the higher nobility or chiefs are drawn and these are entrusted with the affairs of the whole tribe. If the council cannot agree on a chief, one is selected by lot.

In some parts of Morocco an important political device is the alliance in which each segment of a tribe is affiliated with one or two alliances. In this manner feuding within the tribe can be controlled, since if one clan attacks another, this would be the call for the members of the alliance to come to the aid of their brethren. And of course members of the same alliance do not feud with each other. As long as the alliances remain strong, a tribal chief's power is curtailed since booty acquired in fighting has to be shared by all members of an alliance.

Occasionally a tribal chief is able to secure an adequate following with sufficient fire power so that he can impose his will on his tribe and extend it over others. This invariable entails his being able to gain control of the two alliances, and to assassinate rival chiefs as well as to provoke local conflict which he might manipulate to his advantage. After gaining domination over an area he could then seek to reinforce his position by being appointed a *qaid* (agent) by the Moroccan sultan. Whether or not he is able to ascend this far on the ladder of political success, his autocratic rule is usually short-lived. Establishing a dynasty is next to impossible due to the fact that the chief is faced with constant revolt which ultimately becomes successful and returns the system to the old decentralised anarchic order. In any event, the system creates the rudiments of government and a tenuous autocratic state structure. It provides an historical process of cyclic oscillation between archy and anarchy.

Some Moroccan Imazighen have an interesting mediation technique. While minor disputes are left to the local chiefs and councils, major disputes involving members of differing tribes are submitted to 'holy men' or Igurramen. These hereditary saints are ideally descendants of the Prophet and so possess *baraka* or holiness. They have magical powers and are known to be good and pious men. They do not fight, or engage in feuds or litigation, but are non-combatants and permanently neutral pacifists who comprise their own separate patrilineages. They are the mediators between potentially hostile groups. Aside from this task they supervise the election of chiefs among the several tribes in their vicinity, provide sanctuary, protection for strangers and act as centres of information.

An important part of their mediator judicial role is to witness collective oaths. As was mentioned for the Kabyle, the collective oath is deemed effective because one swears on pain of divine punishment should perjury be committed. But Gellner suggests that this is not ultimately the reason for the effectiveness of this method of adjudication, since individuals do perjure themselves. To Gellner the effectiveness of the collective oath is that if a group wishes to stand behind one of its own it will be able to do so; it will swear collectively to the innocence of the alleged culprit. But it can also use the mechanism to punish one of its own who is too much of a trouble-maker, by some or all of his kinsmen refusing to take the oath in which case the plaintiff wins.

The saints are mediators of disputes, not judges, since they cannot enforce their decisions, but depend upon the acceptance of the verdict by those involved. Those who refuse to abide by a verdict face considerable danger due to the moral authority of the saints. Public opinion and especially that of the saints and their clients would be turned against such persons.

In addition to the fact that Imazighen society may be characterised by a hierarchical structure which distinguishes prestigious tribal council members from lesser lights, there is a more clear cut class or even caste-like division. Thus Imazighen have a small population of slaves. In addition tiny communities of Jews have resided in the land and these too have been a subordinate 'pariah' caste. Among some Imazighen, such as those of the desert oases, there has existed a Haratin caste of serf cultivators, usually having distinct Negroid physical features.

In sum, Imazighen style societies are hierarchical, yet in many respects egalitarian. They exhibit anarchic characteristics and also give birth to autocratic regimes. They are suggestive as well of interesting non-governmental techniques for social control. Recent decades, in part because of improved military technology, have brought all Imazighen much more under the direct control of central governments.

The Santals

Several million people in India have been traditionally classed as 'tribal'. This means they belong to those minority ethnic communities which neither observe the caste system nor accept the ideology or ritual of Hinduism. They are egalitarian and ordinarily organised into exogamous patrilineal clans. Tribal people are found scattered throughout India living as village agriculturalists. Their egalitarian ideology and decentralised social system in some cases suggests an anarchic order.

The Santals, at least, have only the barest indication of any governmental system. Numbering over 3,000,000 they live in eastern India, largely in the state of Bihar. In the Santal village life is ordered by one's own kin group (his family and clan) and by the village council and headman. Headmanship is an hereditary position, normally passing from father to son, but nevertheless requiring the approval of the village's household heads. It is an office for life. A headman is seen as the main protector and repository of tradition, which is greatly treasured by Santal. He may be referred to as the 'big man', in other words, a man of considerable influence. He is also seen as a man of wisdom and learning. Nevertheless, he is at best a first among equals. "Publicly he is little more than the voice of consensus, though privately his influence is that of an especially respected and powerful man" (Orans, 21). The headman receives certain tributes and privileges for his role, including rent free lands, a portion of each animal slain on a communal hunt and a central place at all weddings.

There are six other offices in a village and these are by appointment and for life. These include village priests and an assistant responsible for public morals.

The council comprises all household heads in the village. It assembles regularly and under the chairmanship of the headman. While he ordinarily calls meetings, anyone in the village can make a request that one be held. Apparently, in Santal tradition there is strong emphasis upon open and free meetings which guarantee every member the right to express his views fully. The aim of any meeting should be to achieve consensus, but if this unanimity is not forthcoming, the support of the overwhelming majority is accepted. Usually final decisions follow the recommendations of the headsman.

According to Somers, Santal village life is so structured that it prevents concentrations of power. Thus, the seven village office holders are never able to constitute a special power clique because council meetings are held frequently and are open and free. Santal also do not take kindly to the secrecy which would be required for a clique to operate. The village has different foci of power such that they counterbalance the power of the headman. While each institutionalised social segment has authority over its members, there is nevertheless considerable tolerance for individual autonomy. It seems that Santal have a healthy distrust for power and have therefore not only developed techniques to minimise its concentration, but have been diligent in preserving and enforcing them.

Local village affairs are the responsibility of the council and headman. Conflicts between persons of two different villages necessitate settlement through the offices of elders of the village involved. A group of between ten to 20 villages constitutes a territorial confederation and this is the largest unit of political integration in Santal society. This confederation also has a council composed of elders and headmen from member villages. There is no formalised technique for selection of members. One of the members, usually a headman of a village, is elected permanent chairman of the group. This assembly is a 'court of last resort' and is concerned with intervillage affairs. Here also no decisions are made unless consensus of an overwhelming majority has been achieved.

In their adjudications village councils seem primarily to assess fines and order ritual purification as judgements. The aim is to restore peace rather than to punish. Fines are often used to provide a feast and drink for the council and in one area both complainant and accused contribute to such a feast, although the accused gives more.

Apparently for certain offences one could be administered physical punishment (cf. Culshaw). This clearly suggests legal sanctions. Physical punishment and fines are, however, only imposed by the collective meeting of household heads and are arrived at mostly by consensus so that such sanctions are in fact more in the nature of diffuse sanctions. They are not those enjoined by the force of a select elite.

The most awesome punishment which could be imposed on an individual or group is ostracism, which is, of course, one form of diffuse sanctions. This seems largely to be imposed by the council of the confederation and in connection with infractions of marital regulations. A person or a group declared ostracised is first lampooned by the whole community. Then the guilty will be shunned and treated as if non-existent. The sentence of ostracism may be permanent or temporary. In the latter, return to the community may depend on the person's willingness to change his ways, his demonstrated repentence and payment of the costs of purification ceremonies.

Members of Santal society are concerned about concentrations of power and the need to preserve an egalitarian society which gives some free rein to individual expression. There is at the same time a strong dedication to tradition; religious sanctions are both powerful and important. With the emphasis upon consensus of the total community, diffuse sanctions rather than legal sanctions seem to prevail and thus, at the least, Santal society exemplifies a condition of marginal anarchy. Yet, with the imposition of British colonial rule and, more definitely, with the creation of the Indian republic, Santal society has been radically modified and more clearly integrated into and subjugated to the national state. For example, confederational councils have apparently not acted among the Santal since 1947 and local headmen are now responsible to authorities of the central government.

The medieval free city

Another social and cultural milieu upon which Kropotkin looked with considerable favour was the medieval free city commune. He leads us to believe that in its early form it was a society without the state and a community of free men. But how free was it? Did it in fact lack government?

Kropotkin argues that the medieval free city had its origin in the village community and in the notion of the fraternity or guild. "It was a federation of these two kinds of unions, developed under the protection of the fortified enclosure and the turrets of the city."

In some places this was a 'natural growth', in others, especially in Europe, it resulted from revolution. "(I)nhabitants of a borough . . . mutually took the oath to put aside all pending questions concerning feuds arisen from insults, assaults or wounds, and they swore that henceforth in the quarrels that might arise they would never again have recourse to personal revenge or to a judge other than the syndics nominated by themselves in the guild and the city" (Kropotkin, 1943, 19).

The *Encyclopaedia Brittanica* says: "It would be very wide of the mark, however, to imply that the communes were democracies. The life of all the towns was characterised by a struggle for control, as a result of which the wealthiest and most powerful citizens (patricians) were usually more or less successful in monopolising power. Within the communes oligarchy was the norm."

The liberal characteristics of these communes did vary considerably, however not only from place to place, but also the same city might experience a period of relative liberality and, then, ultimately decline into tyranny. Indeed, the latter seems to be the historic process of most of them.

The residents of the medieval commune, as Kropotkin notes, swore a collective oath to follow the decisions of the city's elected judges. However, this collective oath was not always freely given; residents were often forced to make it. In addition, it soon became only a perfunctory act. Judges and other city administrators were chosen, often in a popular assembly, from the wealthy and influential families who were precisely those most interested in having a free city — free of the interference of neighbouring dukes and kings so they might better pursue their business interests. Not only did this situation then create a ruling body of oligarchs, but it enhanced the class differentiation already present.

Kropotkin overlooks the class oriented and exploitive nature of the European guild system. Ostensibly one might say members of a guild gradually progressed from one status to a higher and more responsible one — that the ultimate aim of guild membership was graduation to the rank of master. This then is no different from the ideal of any rational educational system in which the student has the potentiality of becoming equal in knowledge to his or her teacher. However that might be, in the guild system, masters were the rulers and indeed dictators. The apprentices at the bottom were treated hardly better than common slaves. They had to be especially submissive and obedient if they wanted to advance to a higher rank of journeyman, since that depended upon the say of the masters. All power in the guild was vested in the masters and the majority of members could only act as 'yes men' to them. Also the free cities acquired an increasing population of wage working proletarians who had no decision making role in the guilds, or in any part of the economy or polity.

From the point of view of the serf on the feudal estate, the free commune of the medieval period might have seemed like a haven of freedom. And even from the vantage point of a 19th century European the free commune must have stood out as a laudable oasis in a desert of authoritarianism. But there is little justification for Kropotkin's treating it as if it were some worthy example of early anarchy.

Fascist corporatism, syndicalism and the medieval commune

It is interesting to note the occasional close relationship between views which are ordinarily diametrically opposed. Sometimes indeed, opposite views are so opposite to one another that they converge in similarity. Obviously fascism and anarchism have diametrically opposed ideals — particularly about the morality of the state and the role of the individual. Yet, as was suggested early in this essay, the anarchist description of the nature of the state is not always that divergent from the fascist one. The difference, which is crucial and fundamental, is that while the anarchist sees the state as morally wrong, the fascist sees it as right and good. Fascism and anarcho-syndicalism also share a common historical tie to the corporate system allegedly associated with the medieval commune.

Rather ironically a myth of the medieval commune's social organisation seems to have been used as a model for both fascist corporative theory and the anarcho-syndicalist idea of federalism. Presumably the administration of medieval cities was by an assembly of representatives of the several corporations or guilds which constituted the city.

In anarcho-syndicalist theory the free commune myth becomes transformed into an administration by levels of presumably voluntarily confederated bodies representing the various crafts and trades. The top level is either a national or world federation. In fascist theory, which draws not only on the medieval mythic model, but on anarcho-syndicalism as well, the nation state is conceived as a corporation just as the medieval city was viewed as a corporation. Similarly it was to be governed by an assembly of representatives of the several corporations within the state. In fascism this means one segment representing the working force through its syndicates divided according to craft and another segment representing management. The state is seen, in Hobbesean fashion, as the grand arbitrator, ameliorating these forces in the public interest. (Of course, in actual operation the interests pursued were those of the clique controlling the state and secondarily those of business management.) The Soviet system might be seen as a modification of the syndicalist and fascist models. It is certainly closer to the latter since in effect the Soviet system absorbs the corporations of the workers and the capitalists into the state bureaucracy.

In the United States the Catholic Worker movement has for years carried on a campaign for a new society which combines Roman Catholicism with communalism, anarchism and pacifism. It is, however, clear to anyone who has read the *Catholic Worker* and other materials published by their followers that the movement seeks a return to medievalism, a criticism made of the movement almost 40 years ago by the Communist *Daily Worker*. The anarchism of the *Catholic Worker* is a romanticised and nostalgic notion of a medieval free commune. Their model amounts to a variation on an authoritarian corporative one: the church becomes the state.

Anabaptists and anarchy

Kropotkin, in his essay on the origin of the state, mentions the Anabaptist movement as an example of anarchism, although present day members of Anabaptist sects and atheist oriented anarchists would undoubtedly be a little disturbed at such an association. Modern legatees of Anabaptism are the Mennonite, Amish and Hutterite sects. Basic to their teaching is the 'two Kingdoms' theology, which has its roots ultimately in Augustine's *City of God*. To Augustine there are two cities: the earthly city of self love and contempt for God and the heavenly city of love of God and contempt for self. The latter, or city of God, manifests itself on earth in the church. Since the church has elements both of the heavenly and earthly cities, it should not be identified as the city of the God. The state corresponds to the earthly city. A true Christian state works in close relation with the church, promotes the church and secures the peace. Church and Christian state are inextricably bound together in mutual dependence and obligation.

This scheme, which became the model for the medieval conception of church state relations was modified by the Anabaptists. Thus the earthly city or kingdom represented by government and the state is seen as 'worldly' and un-Christian. There can be no such thing as a Christian state or government since it is founded upon the principle of the legitimate use of violence to compel obedience to law. Since violence cannot be used by Christians, they therefore cannot participate in government or in the administration of the state. Furthermore, Christians being right-minded individuals and members of the church, and therefore of the Kingdom of God, have no need for governments. Governments as institutions of the kingdom of this world are for worldly, evil-doing people. As long as there are the latter, governments are necessary. Christians must stand aloof from them to avoid participation in their operation. At the same time they should be obedient to them where it is within their conscience to be so. They should render unto Caesar. Such rendering, however, does not include being a member of a military organisation or a police force. Nor does it mean holding political offices or voting for them or serving on juries, which may send men to prison or to their death.

The true Christian is a member of the Kingdom of God through the earthly organisation of the kingdom, which is the church. This in turn, is the community of believers and of those who practice the teachings of Christ in everyday life. In lieu of secular government, believers are under the guidance of congregations of which they are full, equal and voluntary members. The church is a voluntary contractual association; one does not have to belong. The member is expected to live according to the doctrine and the rules of the church. Such doctrine and regulations are not determined by an elite body of hierarchs, but represent the collective product of the total religious community.

There are, however, clergy who are elected by lot from among the members of the congregation and they lead the church rituals and take a major role in interpreting church doctrine and in dealing with alleged wrongdoers. The ministers and bishops are the men of influence in the community who are at least readily able to sway a large part of a congregation, if not all, to their way of thinking. They do not have the power to make decisions arbitrarily by themselves, however. When a member of a congregation is accused of wrongdoing his or her case is heard by the whole membership and decided by it. The ultimate punishment is 'disfellowshiping' in which the errant member is expelled from membership, which in the close knit highly integrated order of the Anabaptist congregation has always meant a serious punishment. Before a person is given such a sentence, however, he is encouraged to make a public confession before the assembled congregation and ask for forgiveness. Such a request is invariably granted and the matter is ended. Refusal to do so is considered a defiance of the entire church and this defiance of the community ultimately, then, becomes the most serious offence. Disfellowship means not only that one is expelled from membership, but also that one is totally shunned by all the church and cannot share in the religious services. It is in this general manner that Hutterite colonies and Amish congregations operate today. They have no police or courts and do not apply to them, but settle their dispute within their own communities in a system without government or the state, but founded, of course, on the ultimate sanction of God's disapproval. Such a system, as much as others we have discussed, requires firm belief in the power of the supernatural sanctions. It demands such a dependence upon the community of believers that shunning and disfellowship are perceived as excruciating punishment and so are effective deterrents to deviant behaviour. Some so punished would not find it easy to continue in defiance of the congregation and at the same time continue residing among its members.

Unlike the other communities described thus far these Anabaptist groups exist within states, so that they have always been ultimately subject to the law and force of a given government, although as far as they are concerned this would not in any way make their system of social control for themselves any different than if they were not subjects of nation states. Many such groups, for example, the Hutterites, have the characteristics of intentional communities which are discussed below.

Bibliographic note
On ancient Iceland see Durrenberger, Gjerset and Thompson. On the Imazighén see Bourdieu for the Kabyle, Gellner, Hart and Vinogardov for others. See also Munson. Regarding the Santal, see Mukherjea, Orans and Somers. Materials on the medieval free cities were drawn from Clarke, Hughes, Lodge, Martines, Pirenne, Previte-Orton and Rörig. For the Anabaptists see Friedmann and Hostetler.

VII

Anarchy in the Modern World

In the modern world there have been a few isolated attempts at creating the anarchist commonwealth. One type of experiment is the institution of anarchy within a major region or entire country. Another is the small scale communal experiment — the 'utopian' or intentional community established within the existing larger society. In both we are dealing with a set of circumstances different from what has been encountered so far. For here we have self-conscious efforts to establish anarchy by individuals committed to the anarchist ideology of 19th and 20th century Europe and America. This implies not only a rejection of the state and government, but also of church and patriarchy, male dominance and all dominance by elders. It also involves deliberately planning a social order based upon voluntary co-operation.

There are two cases of attempts to institute anarchy at the regional or national level. One is from the Ukraine during the Russian Revolution and the other from Spain during the Revolution or Civil War, 1936-39. Unfortunately, the circumstances in both are muddled because of the prevailing war conditions and therefore cannot provide an adequate idea of an anarchist society in 'normal' times.

Not only did the Ukrainian case occur during the great revolutionary upheaval after 1917, but it was also a short-lived affair. Nestor Makhno, leader of anarchist revolutionary forces in the Ukraine, initially directed his energies against the Czarist army. But for a short period between late 1918 and June 1919, he gained sufficient control of the cities of Ekaterinoslav and Aleksandrovsk, along with the surrounding countryside, for some implementation of anarchist communal ideas to be achieved.

In the rural areas, followers of Makhno expropriated farm lands, livestock and implements from the landed estates as well as from wealthy small holders, leaving their owners, according to Makhno "two pairs of horses, one or two cows (depending on the size of the family), a plough, a seeder, a mower and a pitchfork. . ." With this expropriated property the peasants organised communes. It is alleged that the communes were "created freely, by a spontaneous impulse of the peasants themselves, and with the help of a few good organisers, for the purpose of providing the necessities of life for the working people". Everyone was expected to work while administration and co-ordination of affairs was placed in the hands of those of their number who were deemed most capable, such administrators returning to their ordinary workplace with the other peasants when these duties had been accomplished. Thus there seems to have been an attempt to minimise differences between the workers and the co-ordinators so as to avoid development of a bureaucracy (Voline, 105 ff). According to Voline, the Makhnovist partisan soldiers never exerted any pressure on the peasants.

Makhno himself declared that in the communities members "applied themselves willingly to the task". There were communal kitchens and dining halls, although a member could eat with his or her family in its own quarters without objection. Apparently each member was expected to take a responsible attitude towards food and inform the commune how much was required before taking it. Sundays were days of rest, but if members informed their work mates ahead of time they could leave the commune at other times as well. Overall management of the commune was by a regular meeting of all members.

Makhno reports that there were four of these communes within three or four miles of Gulyai Polya and many more in the surrounding district. A commune apparently had from 100-300 members, each being allotted sufficient land by "district congresses of land committees". Yet a majority of the population of the region was not involved in the anarchist communal movement and even within the communes only a minority were anarchists. The great majority of villagers did not join the communes, "citing as their reasons the advance of the German and Austrian armies, their own lack of organisation, and their inability to defend their order against the new 'revolutionary' and counter-revolutionary authorities" (Avrich, 132). In the urban areas there seems to have been little organisation along anarchist lines. Only a minority of the workers were supporters of Makhno and, unlike the peasants, they had little experience in "managing their own affairs" and "were lost without the guidance of supervisors and technical specialists"

(Avrich, 25) Peasants could also barter produce whereas workers depended wholly on wages.

During this short period, several regional congresses were held by the peasants, workers and partisans of the region. While they were presumably established to co-ordinate a regional economic and social programme, they devoted most of their time to the pursuit of the war, initially against the Czarists but eventually against the Bolsheviks as well. One congress organised a Revolutionary Military Council which was supposed to carry out all decisions of the congresses, but had itself no power to legislate. Makhno claims that "once the resolutions of this Second Congress were made known to the peasants of the region, each new town and village began to send to Gulai-Polya, en masse, new volunteers desiring to go to the front against Denikin" (general of the White Army) (Voline, 109).

These rather ambiguous descriptions by Makhno and Voline of the actual practice raise more questions than they answer. One wonders how many of these army volunteers were truly volunteers. One may ask to what extent individualism in the commune was tolerated. One may question the technique of 'expropriating' property, especially from small holders. Then, too, Makhno's own proclamations have an all-too-familiar ring: "Anyone convicted of counter revolutionary acts or of banditry will be shot on the spot". Persons refusing to accept Soviet, Ukrainian or any other kind of money "will be subject to revolutionary punishment". "All individuals who attempt to hinder the distribution of this declaration will be regarded as counter-revolutionaries" (from Proclamations of the Makhno Movement, 1920 in Avrich, 134).[1] Makhnovist conceptions of justice and freedom seem to have been closer to those of the Bolsheviks than to anarchy. At best it would appear that Makhno and his cohorts sought to initiate a kind of decentralist military democracy which was soon nipped in the bud. Although there were attempts to prevent the development of a differentiation between the bureaucrat and the worker, we might expect that even if the Makhnovist society had survived, that difference would have soon appeared and a red bureaucracy established, as in the Soviet Union as a whole (cf Luciano Pellicani). But the Makhno experiment had so little time

---

[1]At a meeting discussing Makhno this writer inquired how one could be an anarchist and at the same time order people shot for disobeying one's commands. The chief response from anarchists seemed to be: "But Makhno organised workers' and peasants' collectives as well as educational and cultural facilities". And to this the obvious reply is that Mussolini also made the railways run on time.

and was continually harrassed by Czarist and Bolshevik alike that it probably should not be judged too harshly.

The Spanish Revolution
The second example of the attempt to establish an anarchist society in this century occurs in Spain — beginning in 1936. Yet again we have an equivocal situation: is this an attempt to establish a decentralised collectivist democracy or anarchy per se? In writing of the situation Sam Dolgoff, Vernon Richards and other anarchists have considered the movement and the society 'anarchist'. Gaston Leval, who observed many of the collectives directly, prefers to call the movement 'libertarian communism' or 'revolutionary libertarianism' even 'libertarian democracy'.

The Spanish Civil War, which ultimately brought down the Republic and established the Fascist regime of Francisco Franco, is also seen by members of the left and, especially the libertarian left, as a Spanish Revolution. It was considered a revolution because during the period from July 1936 until March 1939, widespread fundamental changes were introduced into the social and economic life of much of Spain. Most important to our interest is the establishment of new social institutions by anarchists.

Spain in 1936 had the largest anarchist movement in the world. Indeed, possibly more than half of all anarchists in the world were Spaniards. This was the precipitate of a well-established tradition which carried a popular anarchist movement back to 1872. The Spanish movement was essentially Bakuninist in that it favoured an organisation of society into localised collectives which would federate into local federations and in turn form broader federations.

An important feature of Spanish anarchism was its mass support both from rural and urban areas. Indeed, anarchist writers such as Rocker and Murray Bookchin have argued that the traditional Spanish peasant community perpetuated a tradition amenable to anarchist collectivism. Bookchin even claims anarchism is 'embedded' in the life of the Spanish people. What this seems to refer to is the pre-capitalist collective and mutual aid practices in the village in addition to individualist values held by the Spanish peasants. This combination of mutualism and individualism is not unique to the Spaniards. It seems to be a common feature of peasant peoples. Certainly the neighbours of the Spaniards, the Imazighen and Arab peasants, might be so characterised. Anarchism might not be so much embedded in the life of the Spanish people, as a certain predisposition to it may be embedded in peasantry and this because of the general character of the peasant situation. Even so, such an observation as Bookchin's does not adequately take into account the authoritarian side of Spanish life, such as the influence of the church and the fact that fascism had some appeal among Spaniards.

Clearly, however, the support for Bakuninist federalism among Spanish peasantry, especially suggests that that milieu when faced with the radical social-technological upheaval of the last 100 years, was a fertile ground for anarchism.

It is not my purpose here to enter into any details of the organisation and operation of the Spanish anarchist collectives, other than to raise some questions concerning the role of authority within them. The ideal of all the communes was to institute a free collective characterised by communal ownership of means of production, voluntary membership and right of withdrawal without punishment, full and equal participation in the decision-making process, free choice of occupation, equal pay, free education, medical care and pharmaceuticals, and the replacement of money by ration or credit cards and an intercommune barter system.

The collectives in Spain, like those in Makhno's Ukraine, operated only during a period of intense hostilities and open warfare. This had the obvious adverse effects of creating shortages of all kinds, and of disrupting communications, effective social intercourse and trade. But it also had the positive effect of continually motivating all members as a united force against a common enemy: it was a fight for survival such that many normal problems, which might have caused conflict in ordinary times, were set aside and overlooked. Not only did the adverse war circumstances affect the system, but within the short span of less than three years it can be questioned whether there was sufficient time for the development of the kinds of oligarchic and bureaucratic arrangements Michels or Machajski, for example, might have predicted as part of the dynamics of such a situation. Finally, it is also worth bearing in mind that in almost all the collectives the dedicated anarchists were invariably in a minority. In most of them, socialists and others not particularly committed to the principles of decentralism, equality and freedom, were a majority.

Reviews such as those of Leval or Dolgoff show that collectives did implement the principle of communal ownership. In the agricultural collectives the land, livestock and implements were the property of the commune. Business appears to have been conducted with maximum participation by members. There were frequent meetings and open discussions. There was an honest attempt to introduce some equalisation in wages for all. Free education, medicine and pharmaceuticals were universal and some collectives went further to provide free housing, electricity and bread.

Nevertheless for a presumed anarchist experiment some important questions arise — again similar to those which come to mind with regard to the Makhno experiment. First, it appears that in their meetings few communes operated according to the principle of consensus, but instead relied on majority vote. Now this may be an appropriate anarchist technique if it is not utilised as a mechanism to oppress a minority point of view. This means in effect that issues of fundamental principle cannot be very easily decided. Further, whatever the case, the minority must always have the right either not to follow the majority will, or to withdraw.

The right to withdraw seems to have been recognised by the Spanish collectives, yet someone who left stood a good chance of thereby losing any contribution to the collective on joining. More important what happened to those people who did leave or for that matter to those who did not wish to join any collective? Presumably one had the choice of belonging to a collective, or remaining an independent worker. In agriculture this meant one was limited to a holding which did not require hired wage labour to operate, since that was forbidden. Leval tells us, in some of the ambiguous terminology of the left, that "through the intermediary of the collective their[1] activities were co-ordinated with the general plan of work". What they produced was sold to the collectives. One is led to wonder in what manner wage labour is forbidden and how the activities of non-collective farmers were 'co-ordinated'. Was there an 'anarchist police force'? Or, in a tradition more amenable to anarchy, were diffuse sanctions such as ostracism or boycotting imposed?

Another questionable grey area is suggested by the mention of committees of collectives which were elected to manage the group's affairs. Collectives quite commonly elected three or so of their number to act as an executive or managerial committee or 'administrative commission', to which seemed to be delegated no small amount of authority. They decided hours of labour and payment to be made; they decided whether or not to expel a member. On the 'libertarian communism' in Alcora village we hear that "(t)he Committee is the *pater familias*. It possesses everything, it directs everything, it deals with everything. Each special desire should be submitted to it. It is, in the last resort, the only judge. One may object that the members of the Committee run the risk

---

[1] ie, persons who did not belong to a collective.

of becoming bureaucrats or even dictators. The peasants have thought of that too. They have decided that the Committee should be changed at frequent intervals so that every member of the village should be a member for a certain period" (quoted in Dolgoff, 144). Yet is such a total delegation of authority anarchy? It might better describe a democratic arrangement in which terms of office are short and limited to one term per person.

These questions and criticisms should not be interpreted as an attempt to belittle the Spanish effort. For these libertarian collectives were, despite their faults, brave, novel and bold experiments in living. Because of their anti-authoritarian bias they were probably the only truly radical large scale efforts at change thus far in this century.

The anarchist intentional community
Intentional communities are in no sense sovereign entities, but quite the contrary, they are communities within and upon the land of sovereign states. They are attempts to initiate anarchic communities 'within the shell of the old'. Thus, for example, the several anarchist communes established in the United States all have had to conform in some fashion to United States law and in many cases have been forced to close down largely because they have not so conformed. Any anarchy in such communities becomes highly circumscribed and is applicable to the internal affairs of the group itself, where even here the long arm of the law may sometimes reach. Any such commune finds itself an integral part of the political and economic system of the state whether it wants to be or not.

Further, individual members themselves have been reared in the cultural traditions and values of that state and have only the greatest difficulty divesting themselves of their delecterious effects. In communes which do survive more than a few years, the children do not have the same desires, motivations and emotional problems as their parents. Children reared in communes will not have the devotion to them and the same ideals as their parents. The charisma of the first generation is succeeded by the routine of the second. Nor can the commune easily shield the young or any others from the formidable 'attractions' of the outside. How to keep them down on the commune is another major problem. In short, from the start, any such project as an anarchist intentional community has an overwhelming chance of failure because of the odds against it which emanate from the external world.

Anarchic communal experiments have always comprised small populations. Indeed, the great majority hardly ever reached

100 permanent members and they have been family-like affairs. Moreover, they are invariably not self-sufficient economically. Some, or most of the members, obtain employment outside in order to sustain the community. While the anarchist experiments have often been based on a communal ownership of the land, full communism, in the sense of a pooling of wealth and labour, has been less common than among other kinds of experiments.

Most of the anarchist intentional communities have been located in the United States and Great Britain. Probably the first which might be characterised as anarchic was founded by Josiah Warren. He was not only one of the great creative thinkers within the anarchist movement, but was also an inventor of gadgets and a social experimenter as well. For most of his life he was interested in the intentional community movement and indeed he lived during its hey day in America — the first three quarters of the 19th century. Warren took part in Owen's Harmony community and left it in 1826 believing that its main problems were a lack of individuality and failure to encourage self-reliance. Warren was an individualist anarchist who did not wish to introduce communism, but advocated a system of free contract in which each would receive according to the time he devoted to his labours. In his Equity Store he tried to implement his ideas by a system of goods exchange based on labour notes, each worth the time in labour devoted to produce an object or to provide some services.

In 1831, Warren, with others, organised a co-operative industrial community in Ohio called Equity. Here it was hoped Warren's ideas on education and social order would be instituted. The basic principle of anarchy was adopted: that one might do as one pleased but always at one's own cost. The experiment however soon failed, not because of internal problems of the community, but because the region was infested with malarial bacteria, making it impossible to carry on after 1835.

Warren did not endeavour to found another community until several years later when he established Utopia, again in Ohio. Here each family purchased its own house and lot and engaged in the equal exchange of labour through notes which were used in all internal community transactions. The economy was primarily industrial, as members engaged in grinding corn and manufacturing wood and iron products. At one time there were almost 100 residents. To Warren, at least, Utopia was designed primarily to demonstrate the practicality of a free community; permanent survival was secondary. And the colony did prosper and operated successfully according to anarchist principles. It eventually suffered from the Civil War and from the attraction of members and

potential members to the cheap land in the west. In the end it
seems to have disappeared by merging into the local scene as
another American community. While there were apparently still
a few of the original members around in 1875 most of them had
moved on to Minnesota and cheaper land some 25 years before.

Finally, Warren was instrumental in establishing a third
community, Modern Times, on Long Island, not far from New
York City. Beginning in 1851, up to three acres of land were sold
to an individual and on this each settler built a house. The chief
economic activity was market gardening. Members largely engaged
in growing fruits and vegetables for the New York City market.
Here as well emphasis was placed on voluntary co-operation,
exchange of labour notes, and a system of education which stressed
self-reliance, freedom and the acquisition of manual arts. By 1854,
37 families resided at Modern Times and it was proving to be a
successful experiment, both economically and politically. Because
of the publicity and easy accessibility to New York City, the colony
received a large number of curious visitors, many of whom decided
to stay on. The community refused to adopt rules which might
prevent individuals from settling within it. Consequently a variety
of eccentrics came to live in Modern Times. While they never
constituted a very significant number, they gave the colony some
adverse publicity. This notoriety, however, was not sufficiently
detracting to inhibit the growing success of the place, in contrast
to some other communes which were practically destroyed by bad
publicity. The Civil War with its economic hardships ultimately put
an end to Modern Times as an experiment in voluntary co-operation
and mutualism.

What is most noticeable about these three communities is the fact
that none of them failed because of their anarchism; all ceased to
exist entirely because of external factors — conditions which would
have crushed any community.

Another anarchist communal experiment was established at
Home, Washington about 20 miles west of Tacoma. The Mutual
Home Association was formed in 1898 and acquired land, the use
rights to which it sold to members in the form of one to two acre
plots. Membership was open to those who sought "the personal
liberty to follow their own line of action no matter how much
it may differ from the custom of the past or present, without
censure or ostracism from their neighbours" and "the placing of
every individual on his or her own merits, thereby making them
independent" (quoted in LeWarne, 171).

The communitarian aspects of Home were extremely limited.
A cooperative for food supplies, a school, library and a variety

of classes and clubs for art, Esperanto, Oriental philosophy, music and physical culture were available. In addition, there was neighbourly mutual aid. Communal property included a meeting hall, a sea wall, sidewalks and a cemetery. As in the Warrenite communities, most activity was left up to an individual's own enterprise.

Membership increased from 54 in 1899 to 213 by 1910 — its largest size. A year later the Home Grocery Association, a co-operative, collapsed amidst a bitter law suit and factional dispute. And by 1917, as a result of a court case, the Home Association itself was dissolved and placed in receivership. One faction claimed the other had usurped the organisation by making crucial changes in the constitution of the organisation without the approval of the other faction.

In Great Britain, during the last decade of 19th century, at least eight anarchist communes were organised. Two of these were influenced primarily by Kropotkin's views, while six were Tolstoyan. They were all extremely small operations, rarely having more than a dozen members. They also had only small acreages with market gardening as the primary economic endeavour. The Purleigh Colony became a centre for the publication of Tolstoy's works which were translated by Aylmer Maude, a member of the colony. It was one of the largest colonies, at one time having at least 65 members.

Within a year or two after its organisation in 1896, the colony was involved in internal conflict over how to select candidates for membership and how to market the Tolstoy translations without becoming overwhelmed by commercialism and profit-seeking. Apparently Purleigh was eventually dissolved as members left, many to join the Dukhobor communities in Canada.

One tiny colony, the Brotherhood Workshop originally established in Leeds and in the course of time moving to several different locations, has managed to survive until the present day.

The Ferrer Colony founded near New Brunswick, New Jersey in 1915 was named after the Spanish anarchist-educator, Francisco Ferrer. It was organised by New York anarchists who continued to commute to work in the city from their communal homes. At the same time they raised vegetables and poultry, but the most significant communal enterprise was the 'modern school', attended mainly by children of colony families, but also by boarders as well. The school like the community was presumably operated according to anarchic principles of freedom and individuality and managed to survive until the Second World War. While the colony had distinct problems with internal dissent and conflict, the actual factor which caused its demise was external. The United States army constructed Camp Kilmer right next door and this created many critical problems with which the colonists found it eventually impossible to cope. Theft and personal safety seem to have been the main issues and the situation encouraged members to move out. Yet Veysey claims that the military intervention probably only speeded a process of already existent slow disintegration anyway.

Joseph Cohen, who had been a member of the Ferrer colony, was instrumental in the attempt to found an anarchist-communist commune in Sunrise, Michigan in 1934. This lasted until 1937 and, as his description suggests, it was an experiment which was harrassed by internal conflict from the beginning. Indeed, the failure of the colony may be seen in part as a justification of anarchist theory since its major problems were organisational. There was an excessive delegation of authority; administrative committees formed cliques and proceeded to act arbitrarily and privily. In addition, this was an agricultural community in which few of the members knew anything whatever about farming. Finally, at Sunrise all property was held in common. This creates a more intense and binding set of social relationships than the loose ties characteristic of some of the experiments already discussed and so creates a situation more vulnerable to conflict.

The 1960s were accompanied by a revival of the intentional community movement. This recent development is probably of far greater proportions than was experienced in the previous wave of communal experimentation between 1820 and 1860. What is more, the types of community which stressed individuality and personal freedom are more noticeable in the recent wave, than in the earlier one. Literally hundreds of anarchic communes have sprung up and disappeared with a few surviving for several years.

As was mentioned above, any intentional community faces great odds from the outset in terms of a variety of external factors which threaten group success. However, the fact that some communes have succeeded in face of these odds indicates there are characteristics internal to the community which are of strategic significance regarding success or failure. Some of these might be the following:

1 *Minimisation of adverse publicity and external interference*
Communities which have practiced eccentric sexual and dress habits, or indulged in the use of drugs and at the same time have openly advertised their behaviour, obviously invite failure by the sanctions of the greater community and police interference. The community which is the least unusual has the best chance of

surviving at the hands of the outside world. While it has been difficult for any community to disappear from the view of the state, today this is almost an impossible achievement.

2 *Screening of members* Much of communal success depends on the building of a congenial group of members and this is enhanced to the extent that persons applying for membership are adequately tested. This, of course, sets up a 'class' distinction between those who have the power to test and admit or reject and those who are the applicants — a condition which has not always been appealing to libertarians. Nevertheless, a survey of communal experiments indicates how often a major cause of failure has been an inadequate control over admission to membership. On the other hand, the most successful communal movement of all, the Hutterites, has the most stringent admission requirements and practically never admits members from outside.

3 *Individual responsibility* Many a community has failed because of the lack of sufficient numbers of mature and responsible members and a surfeit of what some would call selfish, little kids. It bears repeating that anarchy depends upon the extent to which each member assumes a conscientious, personal responsibility and a sense of self reliance. Riesman refers to such individuals as being 'inner directed' and I suspect that the successful anarchist commune is composed mainly of these kinds of people. Many of the more enduring anarchist experiments have been among those whose cultural milieu was nineteenth century, English and Protestant — an inner directed type. Many Spanish anarchists were as well. At least they often embraced an atheist "puritanism" which opposed alcohol, bullfights and sexual promiscuity (see Hobsbawm, 82, and Brenan, 157). Brenan also saw parallels between Spanish anarchist gatherings and revivalist meetings. There is a relationship between "puritanism" and inner directedness since self discipline among other things is basic to any "puritanism". This is not to say, however, that one must be a puritan in order to be self-disciplined. It would be interesting to determine the extent to which an association between inner directedness and an anarchic polity occurs outside of the European milieu, among the other people which have been discussed in the preceding pages.

4 *Technical capability* The most common ideal for a community has been a rural, subsistence farming colony. In some regions of marginal economic value, these communities have been a qualified success and have even contributed to a modest economic revival of the area. Yet more frequently, they have been economic disasters because members are unfamiliar with either farm or rural life. Failure is most certain when members are not only

ignorant of such life, but persist in naive romantic notions about it.

5 *Communality* To maximize the extent of communal life — communal property, communal eating, communal housing, etc, — tends also to intensify certain problems of conflict. Drawing people of varying backgrounds together and so tying them to one another, engenders trouble. Hutterites have been reasonably successful in a communal venture in good part because they have tried to insure maximum cultural homogeneity of all members. They have strictly controlled the indoctrination of members from the cradle to the grave. At the same time they have a tradition which is nearly half a millenium old. Those anarchist communities of the 19th and 20th centuries which have had some degree of success were 'loosely' structured with a minimum of communal property, communal eating, communal housing, etc — they were neighborhoods of like-minded individuals who were not so intimately involved with each other. There was a broad leeway for individual action and autonomy, yet at the same time mutual aid was always available on call and, of course, economic differences were absent.

Bibliographic note
On Makhno and the Ukrainian movement see Avrich and Voline. Material on the Spanish Revolution is derived from Brenan, Dolgoff, Leval and Richards. On the anarchist intentional communities see Martin for Warren's experiments, LeWarne for the Mutual Home Association, Hardy for the English communes, Veysey for the Ferrer Colony and Cohen, Joseph for Sunrise.

VIII

Do Anarchic Politics have a Message?

Some general characteristics of anarchic polities
Almost all hunting and gathering societies of which we have any
record are egalitarian and anarchic, having no government or state.
A small minority — typically those of the Northwest Coast of
America and of northern California — are rank societies, which
nevertheless frequently lack any governmental system. Among
horticulturalists the extent of egalitarian and anarchic polities is
still widespread, but less so than among hunter-gatherers. On the
other hand, probably a minority of pastoral societies and hardly any
agricultural ones, fall into this category. Among the latter, societies
are characterised by stratification and the state.

The egalitarian quality of any polity, anarchy included, it must
be remembered, is to be seen within the context of same sex and
general age or generation. True sexual equality is a rarity and
societies which approach it are, like the Ifugao or Dayaks, more
often than not those which have a bilateral kinship system. With it
there is a lack of differentiation or preference regarding relatives
through either parent; there is an equality or an approximate
equality in terms of inheritance through either parent and by
members of either sex. Husband and wife will tend to bring to the
new household equal amounts of property. This bilateral situation
usually sets the stage for relatively equal participation within the
economic sphere (eg, Ifugao, Inuit, Samek). Matriliny sometimes
appears inferior to bilaterality in its ability to provide the most
secure basis for a relative sexual equality. This is because in it,
males are often motivated to neutralise the principle of inheritance
through females by asserting their own dominance.

Anarchy correlates with 'folk' or *gemeinschaftlich* characteristics.
It is easiest where the population of the maximal effective social

group is small — probably up to 200 individuals. In it 'face to face' relations prevail and thus the typical diffuse sanctions of gossip, ostracism and the like can operate most effectively. Anarchy is easiest where the population is homogeneous and undifferentiated. Among other things this means there is only a minimal division of labour and specialisation of task. Such a situation where people are much the same, reduces or minimises the opportunities for differences of opinion, sharp cleavages, and conflict, and maximises what people have in common so that even if there is disagreement there is still immense pressure to conform and keep the system going. Numerous bonds of commonality bind the dissident to the group and prevent total alienation.

Some may interpret these conditions as rigidly curtailing freedom. Freedom, it may be said, is measured by the number of choices open to an individual. And there are obviously fewer choices open to members of these small scale societies. But perhaps we should question how much less freedom exists in such societies if all the members are unaware of a greater number of alternatives and if the same few alternatives are available to all. How, indeed, would such societies compare to those more 'modern' ones in which there are presumably so many more choices, but in fact they are not freely available to everyone?

While it may be said that anarchy occurs most frequently in a small group situation and is probably easier to perpetuate in this condition, this is not to say that it is impossible in a modern more complex context. Rather it is more correct to say that it is not very probable. Yet we do have examples of anarchic polities among peoples such as the Tiv, Lugbara, Nuer and Tonga, numbering in the hundreds of thousands and with fairly dense populations, often over 100 people to the square mile. Such social orders may be achieved through a segmentary lineage system which as we have seen already has certain parallels to the anarchist notion of federalism. Or, as among the Tonga and some East African pastoralists, large populations may be integrated by a more complex arrangement which affiliates the individual with a number of cross cutting and bisecting groups so as to extend his or her social ties over a wide area. In other words, individuals and groups constitute a multitude of interconnected loci, which produce the integration of a large social entity, but without any actual centralised co-ordination.

Even within Western civilisation we have cases of large acephalous organisations. Studies of recent social movements in the United States have led students of such phenomena to speak of segmented polycephalous idea-based networks (SPINs). "An organisation chart of a S P (I) N would look like a badly knotted fishnet with a multitude of nodes or cells of varying sizes, each linked to all the others either directly or indirectly" (Hine, 19). SPINs have no single leader, but each segment has its leaders although none has any authority. Leadership is based upon ability and persuasiveness alone. What holds the various autonomous segments together and prevents disintegration is a wide range of 'horizontal linkages' and most important of all, an ideological linkage. That is, there is much overlapping of membership so that one person belongs to several groups within the whole movement. There is considerable interaction between leaders of the participating groups or cells and leaders themselves may lead in one group and be ordinary members in another. There is also much ritual activity in the form of demonstrations, rallies and the like which draw all together. The real glue of the movement is ideological: a deep commitment to a very few key and basic tenets which are shared by all. Hine suggests that the biological analogue of a SPIN is the earthworm. But another may be the brain within which there is co-ordination of a myriad cells without any 'ruler'.

SPINs are purely instrumental and pragmatic, when the idea which spawns one loses its influence, either because it has been won, or lost, or made obsolete, the SPIN changes or disappears. It is probably significant to anarchist and other propagandists that SPINs do not emerge as a result of rational planning, but "emerge out of functional necessity" (Hine, 20). The parallel of SPINs to Tonga and other like forms of social organisation is obvious. A free society modelled along such lines may prove to be the most resistant to the growth of oligarchy and hierarchy.

Anarchists have frequently also referred to other examples of systems which do work without any head. Thus, we have the European railway system, composed of several independent national rail lines, which co-ordinate their activities so as to allow for efficient passage of goods and passengers amongst several different countries. It is a system without a head. The United States railways are owned and directed by several separate companies which co-ordinate their operations by means of voluntary associations of companies so as to provide for travel throughout the country. The international postal system is of the same acephalous nature.

It is somewhat ironic that certain defenders of a powerful national state are at the same time advocates of an economy which not only lacks a centralised control at the international level, but also has none at the national level. The old liberal capitalist notion that an economy is, or ought to be, a self-regulating system controlled only by the demands of a free market, is in its essence an anarchist notion. However, it no longer remains one when it becomes a guise for exploiting and oppressing others. In any case these several examples are what Bohannan has referred to as 'multicentric' power systems.

It is clear that large, relatively complex social systems or relationships can function efficiently in an anarchic fashion. It is, however, noticeable that none of the ethnographic cases available suggest the operation of anarchy where there are major urban agglomerations. Except for the brief Spanish and Ukrainian experiments, wherever anarchy obtains it is in a rural context. Still, if anarchy can function in a densely populated rural area, there is again the possibility that it could operate in cities as well.

The fact that there are few anarchic polities among complex social structures may mean that the centralised state has appeared to be a more practicable mechanism by which to maintain social relations in such a milieu. It may also mean that certain individuals with power are able to anaesthetise the populace into believing their authority is indispensable and that life is easier by abdicating responsibility to them. The ruled are instilled with the notion that government knows best; it is the most efficient vehicle for providing services to the community, while the ordinary folks are neither qualified nor capable. Like any successful institution, government also prospers by inculcating its necessity in the populace. Once power has been accumulated into a few hands it is more difficult to get rid of it. It has a savage appetite and the habit of a cancer, ever expanding and enlarging. As we have suggested elsewhere in this essay there has been, over the decades, a gradual erosion of self-help and voluntary co-operative institutions in our society, an erosion which has favoured an increasing encroachment of government into the lives of all. This is not only to be criticised as a threat to liberty, but it is equally a threat to the everyday practice of voluntary co-operation, of self-reliance and mutual aid between 'natural' groups in society.

Even if we set aside the real possibility that the masses have been drugged by those who achieve power, we might consider that people's weighting of human values have too often been such that they elect security over freedom, order over liberty and efficiency over individuality. The plain fact is that anarchy requires work, responsibility and a big gamble. Especially today, the majority of people are content to abdicate responsibility to government — perhaps because they are too lazy and because they have been happily mesmerised by those in power; perhaps, also, because their self-confidence has been undermined by the powerful.

Cultural florescence and anarchy

In *Nationalism and Culture* Rudolf Rocker explored the hypothesis that wherever there is a state, there is an inhibition of human cultural develpment and, correlatively, wherever political integration is weak and limited to small groups cultural 'progress' occurs. By culture Rocker refers to the various arts: architecture, painting, music, literature, philosophy. Unfortunately he fails to make any systematic analysis of cultural contents or to disengage the subject from the most subjective level. He makes only personal judgements about the value of Roman literature or of Greek sculpture, for example. Obviously, this is an area in which objectivity could hardly be achieved. An equally serious problem is that Rocker seems to view with approval the ancient Greek city state, the early Spanish commune and the small principalities of 17th and 18th century Europe. It is not clear then whether he is critical of the state or critical only of big states. Whatever the case might be, the argument that cultural florescence is suffocated by the state is a fascinating question, but one replete with too many pitfalls to be answered in any convincing way.

To pursue properly Rocker's question we would require a more precise conceptualisation of the state and above all we would need an objective technique by which evaluation of art forms in different cultures could be made. This formidable task I have no intention of pursuing. A L Kroeber in *Configurations of Culture Growth* attempted something of this sort. He made no evaluations of art forms, but used the names of noted persons as indices for plotting the rise and decline of the several arts and sciences in the major civilisations of the world.

His aim was to determine regularities in the growth of intellectual and aesthetic endeavours in the course of time and from one major civilisation to another. His technique is by no means beyond reproach. And in his conclusions, unlike others such as Spengler or Toynbee, Kroeber finds no grand pattern or patterns, no historical universals. He finds no significant interrelationships between the climaxes of particular configurations, whether these be in the natural sciences, philosophy or arts. Nor are there connections between culmination in a given art and a total cultural climax. The crest of a scientific wave may come before, with, or after that of a literary wave and so on. Cultures often have great climaxes in some arts and sciences and none at all in others. More directly as a response to Rocker, Kroeber finds configurations and their culminations are not particularly related to such factors as the lack or extent of political integration. Both Kroeber and Rocker are only concerned with literate civilisations. One wonders how Rocker, for example, would have looked upon the cultural development among the anarchic polities discussed in this essay, compared to others which have states.

For one thing, we have noted that in such governmentless societies there are nevertheless numerous oppressive features which would seem to inhibit free creative expression. What is more, the atmosphere of freedom in and of itself is insufficient for cultural florescence. The free do not create in a vacuum. It is sometimes pointed out that the Australian aboriginal hunter has much time to think and create, but the end product is not that impressive. Aside from freedom, one requires the appropriate stimulation. The accumulation of knowledge is a certain spur to that stimulation. As one gathers more data one's understanding is eventually enhanced. New connections and relationships are seen; greater insight is achieved and new hunches or intuitions flash into one's mind. The specialisation of task is a major factor in producing a creative atmosphere, because there is the opportunity for a number of individuals interested in the same specific problem to exchange ideas, work together and so inspire each other. Such inspiration is accelerated as one has easy and free communications around the world with others of like concerns. Now *historically*, specialisation of task in the division of labour — the building up of a community of scholars or artists — is invariably associated with some urban development and the creation of a leisured class. This suggests, then, a stratified society which has little place for anarchy.

No one can deny that some degree of personal freedom and individuality is essential for innovation and cultural florescence. But contrary to Rocker it seems that cross cultural analysis and history tell us that humans can be creative under quite dissimilar circumstances. The quantity of freedom which may be essential is highly variable. Certainly no one can argue that the various anarchic polities will have greater developments in the arts simply because they have no state.

Techniques for maintaining order

Freedom and individuality as enunciated in the anarchist movement are European, if not bourgeois, values which grew out of the Protestant Reformation and have roots further back in Greek cultural tradition. Most of the people with which we have dealt maintain an anarchic system and display certain individualist traits but do not commonly explicate philosophical thoughts on freedom. As a matter of fact we may well be valuing these peoples for reasons important to us, but not to them (cf. Colson, 1974, 62 3).[1]

A society may be free of governors, policemen, jails and law — the whole apparatus of government — but this by no means guarantees it will be a free and egalitarian society. The reliance of anarchic polities upon diffuse and religious sanctions may lead to tyranny. The taunts, the gossip, the ostracism and the physical violence which form part of such sanctions often appear unyielding, unforgiving and cruel. And as we know from our small town life there is little place of refuge from such sanctions, so long as one desires to remain within the community. Diffuse sanctions are often difficult to control and can readily get out of hand, as with the vigilante committees of the Old West. What is more, they may be a force of conservatism, stupidity and intolerance. Nevertheless, we who dwell in state dominated societies not only must submit to diffuse sanctions but also the overwhelming power of the state as well. And in our age of sophisticated technology, particularly in the realms of communication, transportation and electronic surveillance, the state has access to an incredibly awesome power. The real tyrannies in this world have been and are state tyrannies.

Anarchic techniques for maintaining order stress self-help and self-regulation, which from the point of view of an American or European may sometimes appear like a perpetual resort to violence in the form of the feud. Lee has addressed the question of relative homicide rates amongst San as compared to the United States and other areas. He calculated the San rate at 20.3 per 100,000 person years. In the United States there are 9.2 homicides per 100,000 population while a study of 23 Ugandan peoples showed a range of between 1.1 and 11.6 per 100,000 with a mode of four to six. The U.S. figures would be far higher if its medical facilities were as rudimentary as those of the San. Moreover, it is noted that many automobile and other accidents in the United States are intentionally homicides but are not counted as such. Far more important is the number murdered in warfare and none are counted in the homicide rate. Consequently Lee revises the American figures and estimates the proper rate in the United States to be about 100 per 100,000. He also figures British, French, and German numbers would be equally as large. However, I would suspect that his estimates are too high. Nevertheless, his conclusions are valid, namely, that San homicide rates are probably quite a bit less than those in the United States

---

[1] In their drive to build modern nation-states and ape the Europeans, Africa's political elites are eager to bury the archaic anarchic elements, or to convert them into the idiom of democratic statism. Old African anarchic decentralism becomes in their hands an example of some ancient African tradition of democratic government and communalism.

and that while the state may be effective in reducing certain kinds of violence such as individual fights, it creates new forms such as war (Lee, 398-399).

Our survey of anarchic polities shows how widespread is the presumed reliance upon the feud, which can be so wasteful of life in its apparent senseless murder and mayhem. What is more, the feud provokes a prolonged state of anxiety and psychological turmoil. However, it is well to bear in mind that the destruction of the feud in an anarchic polity is hardly likely to approach that of the warfare which is conducted between states. While there are no available comparative figures, there is at least one basic difference between feuding and the nature of war which helps substantiate this conclusion. That is, feuds aim at evening a score. The operating thesis is an eye for an eye. They do not aim at annihilation of an enemy or unconditional surrender of the opponent. Often, once someone has been injured in a feud, the fighting stops. At least active peace negotiations will be initiated because of the priority of the maintenance of group harmony. It is essential in any conflict to restore that harmony as soon as possible. Litigation of any kind is not aimed at finding blame for blame's sake, but in satisfying disputants and bringing peace. This entails a central role for third party mediators or go-betweens. These respected men consult with opposing sides until some compromise can be reached. The success of such ventures depends on the ability of the mediator and on the sense of moral obligation to play the game on the part of the parties involved.

Elizabeth Colson believes, however, that it is not so much actual feuding, but fear of provoking a feud, that is an important mechanism of social control in acephalous societies. She refers to recent reviews made independently by E. Adamson Hoebel and Sally Falk Moore which conclude that there is not a great deal of evidence for feuding as such, but a great deal of evidence for fear of the feud. In anarchic polities everyone becomes very much aware of the potential consequences of rash behaviour. Each person learns the need for self-restraint. ". . . (S)ome people live in what appears to be a Rousseauian paradise because they take a Hobbesian view of the situation: they walk softly because they believe it necessary not to offend others whom they regard as dangerous" (Colson, 1974, 37). "There *is* 'peace in the feud' as Gluckman has said, but it is a peace based on the prevention of the first act rather than on the force which leads to the final settlement" (Colson, 1974, 43).

It has been suggested that people in anarchic polities have less to quarrel about because there is less property and much homogeneity and equality. But perhaps again restraint is important because of the fear of consequences, so that there appears to be less quarreling (Colson, 1974, 43).

An obligation to play the game is elemental to the functioning of any anarchic polity. And, of course, it is readily enforced by fear of diffuse and religious sanctions. Nevertheless, those who are used to living in a society governed by policemen and legal sanctions often fail to appreciate the significance of the sense of obligation to play the game as a motivating force for social order even within their own society. We must not forget that in all human societies most members chose to follow the rules because they want to and because they believe in them. They would resist any attempt to lead them into non-conformity. In any society, sanctions of whatever kind are for the tiny minority. Were all law enforcement to be removed tomorrow there would probably be an initial burst of crime, but after the novelty wore off it would dissipate. At the same time, the vast majority would not be involved, but would go about its business as usual. To hold, as some apparently do, that were the law to be removed there would occur some momentous explosion of brutish and murderous behaviour among all the populace is, in the first place, grossly to overestimate the present power of the police. More importantly, it is grossly to underestimate the years of conditioning about right and wrong to which all have been exposed and the power of the internalised censor or conscience.

In those cases where traditional techniques for social control have been removed suddenly or greatly relaxed, two consequences are noteworthy. One is the extent to which voluntary mutual aid spontaneously appears and spreads — people begin helping each other. The other consequence is the opposite response — the one the 'law and order' supporters would predict. That is, there is rioting, looting and mayhem. But the reason for this reaction is not because there is no police to keep order. The reason is suggested by the kinds of people who engage in such behaviour. These peple are definitely not the members of society who have prospered from it, nor are they the ones in positions of prestige, power and influence: On the contrary, they are always from the ranks of the disadvantaged and frustrated. And the revolt — which is what it is — is an attempt at catharsis, to relieve pent up aggression and hostility generated by a system perceived to be oppressive (whether it is 'in fact' oppressive is beside the point; it is seen to be such and that is what counts).

It is an error to think of humans as 'naturally' good; it is equally erroneous to condemn them as monsters. And radicals, of all people, should appreciate the extent to which people are conformists.

Some criticise anarchy because its only cement is something of the order of moral obligation or voluntary co-operation. But democracy, too, ultimately works in part because of the same cement. And it works best where the cement is the strongest. That is, democracy ultimately does not operate only because of the presence of a police force. The free elections and two-party system could never survive if they depended upon the army and the police to enforce them. They survive because participants have a belief in the system and a feeling of obligation to play according to the rules. Hocart has said that government depends on "spontaneous and incessant goodwill. . . Without it governments would collapse" (129).

De la Boetie, Machiavelli and Spooner among others would add however, that in any system of government submission is induced by fear and fraud. In *The Politics of Obedience: The Discourse of Voluntary Servitude* Etienne de la Boetie devotes himself entirely to the question of why people submit to rulers. He makes the following points:

1   People submit because they are born serfs and are reared as such.

2   People are tricked into servitude by the provision of feasts and circuses by their masters and because they are mystified by ritual practices and religious dogmas which aim to hide the vileness of rulers and imbue reverence and adoration as well as servility.

3   The 'mainspring' of domination is not physical force so much as it is a chain effect: the ruler has five or six who are his confidants and under his control; they in turn control 600 and these in their turn control 6,000. "The consequence of all this is fatal indeed. And whoever is pleased to unwind the skein will observe that not the six thousand but a hundred thousand, and even millions, cling to the tyrant by this cord to which they are tied. According to Homer, Jupiter boasts of being able to draw to himself all the gods when he pulls a chain" (78).

Also suggestive of why people obey is Lysander Spooner's classification of "ostensible supporters of a constitution": knaves, dupes and those who see the evil of government but do not know how to get rid of it or do not wish to gamble their personal interests in attempting to do so.

In anarchy there is no such delusion for there is a priority placed upon individual freedom which is absent in democracy. Democracy — granted its concern for liberty and individualism — nevertheless like any other system of rule, puts its ultimate priority in the preservation of the state. When in a democracy one group threatens to withdraw — to secede — there is always the final recourse to a 'war measures' act to compel compliance and suppress 'rebellion'. To summarize, order in the anarchic polity, is founded in diffuse sanctions. It is maintained through self-help, self-regulation and self-restraint and these devices are channelled by fear as well as by the motivation to make the system work and to play the game with a minimum of friction.

Group decision-making
Part of the democratic myth is the sanctity of majority vote. That every so many years each voter goes to the polls and chooses a leader by majority, and the secret ballot is the most sacred ritual of democrats. Anarchists have argued that this is no true indication of liberty. Rather, again as de la Boetie might have observed, the election of rulers by majority vote is a subterfuge which helps individuals to believe that they control the situation. The voter, in fact, chooses from a pre-selected group and invariably there is no choice between contrasting ideologies. The difference between major parties — those that have a chance of victory — in any western country today is no greater than the difference between factions within the Communist party in the Soviet Union or China. No one could seriously argue that there is any ideological or any other enduring traditional philosophical contrast between the major parties in the United States or in Canada. In addition electors might be reminded that they are selecting individuals to do a task for them and they have no guarantee that it will be carried out as they desired. Above all, this job in its essence is one of forcing obedience. Electing men to public office is like being given a limited choice of your oppressors.

Quite often election by majority does not even occur. A candidate for office is elected because he or she has more votes than any single other candidate and actually receives much less than a majority of the votes cast. In addition, the number of people who don't vote — the silent majority — is never taken into account. Presumably a goodly proportion of the non-voters are not particularly enamoured of any candidate. In 1976 in one American state, Nevada, voters were given the alternative in the Presidential election of marking an X beside 'None of the above' — the nearest thing to an anarchist vote. Slightly less than three per cent of those who voted made this choice. In addition, 40-50% never bothered to vote.

We frequently hear the refrain: If you don't vote you have no right to complain. Such an argument makes the false assumption that an election provides real choices. And, of course, it falsely assumes the legitimacy of the process itself: that an individual is required to delegate authority to an arbitrarily chosen few, or that an individual is required to elect his or her own jailers.

Above all, there is the fundamental moral question about the sanctity of the majority. Democracy, in its advocacy of majority rule, attempts to provide an alternative to the rule of one or of a few, but it often replaces that kind of dictatorship by one of the majority or, most commonly, of the plurality. It assumes that right and wrong, that morality, is determined by a majority of those who bother to vote. Ibsen's *Enemy of the People* is a vivid dramatisation of some of the consequences of relying upon majorities. Yet even aside from the fact that minorities may know better, or have right on their side, there remains the truth that the majority compels the minority to conform.

The anarchic polities which we have considered, as well as anarchist theoreticians, have stressed an alternative decision-making device — that of consensus. An issue is argued out until everyone agrees or acquiesces to a given solution, or, in lieu of such agreement, the matter is set aside, usually to be taken up at a later date. The Society of Friends (Quakers) in our own cultural tradition has long practiced this technique as a means of conducting business. Decisions depend upon coming to a sense of the meeting: a point when there is no further expressed opposition to a plan of action.

There are many arguments against this approach. It invariably entails a considerable amount of talk. Indeed, a member of an anarchist intentional community once said that the main product of his group was talk. But there is nothing more human than talk and as long as people engage in it they will not engage in violence. Consensual politics is most commonly criticised on the grounds that business could well be hamstrung by a stubborn minority. This is sometimes the case, but this can also occur in a democratic legislature, which can be as inefficient and time consuming. If one wants an efficient system one would probably do best to appoint a select committee of technocrats to plan and expedite legislation, but this would not be a free society; it would be Orwell's 1984 world.

A more credible criticism of consensual politics derives from the manner in which it tends to work out in actuality. First, consensual politics is effective with small groups, since it depends upon full and open discussion of issues in a kind of face to face relationship. Secondly, in practice there is no equal participation by everyone. Rather the people of influence in the community impress their opinions upon others so that individuals fall in line and at least come to a tacit agreement. Indeed the people of influence in a community may often confer ahead of time and agree to a position for public consumption. Anyone 'holding out' and preventing consensus is ordinarily 'prevailed upon' by influential individuals to see the 'error' of his or her ways. All these kinds of political manoeuverings are equally as common in democratic and other politics. The advantage of a consensual system is that ideally it is morally superior to others in protecting minority rights. Clearly it can become an unwieldy and coercive instrument. Anarchists themselves, in their implementation of communes and collectives, have often found it necessary to resort to the democratic system of majority vote.

An alternative to consensus is decision by lot. Election of ministers and other church officers among the various Anabaptist sects has often been by this process, in the belief that one must avoid the possibilities of strife, which might come from the partisan politics of majority vote elections, and leave the decision up to God who presumably expresses himself in the lot. Election by lot assumes, however, a high degree of group homogeneity, or at least some kind of control over who are to be the potential candidates. One can imagine what would occur if, in the United States, one of the candidates in a lot was a Communist and he was in fact selected.

The search for a decision-making process which is both moral and efficient must yet continue. At least in the smallest more homogeneous group, or in one committed to the priority of group harmony, the consensus technique seems more advantageous.

Types of leaders in anarchic polities

From a review of anarchic polities, different kinds of leadership and attitudes towards leadership emerge. In most cases leadership is looked on positively and to become a 'chief' is an aspiration of the many. There are, however, a minority of societies in which it is considered impolite or unethical to strive for paramountcy in any way. Leadership roles are deemphasised and are not quite approved. Yet, whatever the attitude, leadership patterns in any group do emerge and we may note at least four different types amongst anarchic polities:

1 The Big Man,
2 The Technician,
3 The Holy Man,
4 The Old Man.

The Big Man is the one who acquires a central position of influence in the community and a following of clients as a result of his wealth, his ability to persuade and to orate and, occasionally, because of his physical prowess. Here is the Yurok or Northwest Coast Indian 'chief'. Here also is the Big Man of New Guinea.

The Technician achieves paramountcy especially in hunter-gathering societies. Thus one who is a good hunter collects around him a following which is willing to do his bidding and be fed, as among Athabascan Indian bands of the Canadian Sub-Arctic or among the Inuit. Modifications of this role are found among the San and Pygmies. And the Samek headman is a master technician for a pastoral people.

The Holy Man, through some religious ideology, is accepted as a prestigious person to whom all voluntarily defer, particularly as a mediator of disputes. Here we have the Nuer leopard skin chief or the maraboutic families and lineages of the Imazighen. Also of a slightly different order is the Inuit shaman who acts not so much as mediator, but as a manipulator of people, often for his own ends (a role which mixes the Holy Man and Big Man concepts).

The Old Man is the leading member of the community simply by being the senior male member of the kin group. While the Big Man and the Technician are more frequently achieved statuses and the Holy Man may be either an achieved or an ascribed one, that of the Old Man is ascribed, although even here there may be the slight element of achievement. Thus some elders may be more pre-eminent because of ability in speech, having more wives, more wealth, more sons, or knowledge of ceremony and esoteric doctrine. The Old Man syndrome is characteristic of Australians and particularly of the African horticultural societies. (Tiv, Lugbara, Konkomba, Tallensi, etc.). Some segmentary patrilineal systems combine the Old Man and the Holy Man syndromes, as with the Arab Bedawin.

Earlier it was noted that authority might be considered as rational or irrational. In connection with the above four kinds of leadership it would appear that only the Technician represents a rational form. The others also have clear elements of rationality, but have at the same time irrational or arbitrary qualities. This is most true of the role of the Old Man.

In Max Weber's classification of types of authority, both Big Men and Holy Men fall into the 'charismatic' type, while Old Men combine the gerontocratic and patriarchal attributes of 'traditional' authority. Weber does not really make provision for the Technician (Weber, 324 ff).

Conservative theory holds that the tribute offered the ruler is fully reciprocated by the services of the ruler to the people. This argument has been challenged by persons from a broad spectrum of ideologies, from the democrats to anarchists. Indeed, it seems only the height of self-delusion to contend that all forms of rulership are reciprocal. How could the relationship between an ancient Egyptian peasant and a pharoah conceivably be seen as a reciprocal one? Where is the reciprocity in the enormous wealth which is yearly handed over to the British royal family and the positive services it presumably offers? Does not every ruler acquire special privilege and an essentially non-reciprocal relationship with clients or subjects? Indeed, we may, with Pierre Clastres, say that another way of defining rule is as a non-reciprocal relationship. The ruler is the paramount example of that status.

Henry Orenstein discusses two types of asymmetrical reciprocity: the centripetal and centrifugal. The first is the leader as servant and is best exemplified in Pierre Clastres' analysis of South American Indian chiefs. Here it will be recalled the chief's advantage is seen as a breaking of the fundamental law of social relationships — reciprocity — resulting in a suspicion of power and a desire to contain it. Paradoxically, the chief is contained by his own asymmetrical reciprocity: his excess of wives places him in perpetual debt to the community, so that he must forever be a servant of the people and can never affirm coercive power as a true ruler. This conception of the centripetal 'chief' works against governmental and state organisations.

Orenstein thoroughly confuses the issue when he suggests that centripetal leaders and rulers include such widely variant persons as a South American Indian chief, a Roman emperor and the elected official in a democracy. If this were in fact true, it would make the concept of centripetality useless and meaningless. The centripetal leader is correctly a leader within the most pristine of anarchic polities: he is a servant whose clientele may, if they choose, ignore him with impunity. What democratic elected official or Roman emperor could ever be ignored? Even the command of the justice of the peace must be obeyed on pain of punishment.

In centrifugality the ruler or leader maintains a type of relationship which can command obedience and services. What we have called the Big Man and the Holy Man ordinarily have centrifugal relationships. It is out of this kind of context that we have the creation of the despot and of government. But before exploring this issue further, I would like to suggest that perhaps some types of leaders in anarchic polities are neither centripetal nor centrifugal. Perhaps leaders of certain polities only engage in the ordinary reciprocal relations of everyday people. Consider leadership among the Pygmies. Here it seems to be only of a temporary sort, highly amorphous and 'multicentric', always surrounded by a reluctance to lead or to be aggressive. There seems to be no special advantage to be derived from leadership and the leader is not indebted to his people. The Pygmy leader appears to embody the best anarchic ideal, because he minimises leadership characteristics and retains normal reciprocal relationships with others.

On the origins of the state

As we have seen from our survey of anarchic polities, the seeds of
tyranny and government are readily observable in the performance
of many leaders. The Tiv, Lugbara and other African polities, as
well as the Australians exemplify the potential tyranny of Old Men.
The patriarchal system, it might be argued, does have a certain
rationality, in that it is the elders who have lived the longest and
so presumably have acquired the most experience in living, as well
as having had the greatest opportunity to learn the wisdom of the
ancestors. But it is irrational in that it assumes that all those in
'elder' status are automatically always superior.

By its nature the old man syndrome *alone* cannot perpetuate an
elite power group as a dynasty. A man assumes power as an older
person and retains it for a few short years at which time he must yield
to new persons who were his subordinates. Indeed, in an age graded
society such as the Tiv, a man assumes leadership for a short span
of a decade, when he must retire to inactivity and now find himself
in a social setting where those who were his subordinates are now
leaders. Another reason patriarchy in this anarchic setting may not
lead to government per se is that the entire system is intimately
attached to kinship. Patriarchs or elders are always grandfathers of
some kind. One is not obligated to obey those one does not address
with a paternal type kin term.

The germ of state development might find a more fertile location
in the role of the Big Man. In New Guinea this leader acquires
a body of clients which he is able in some cases to command.
Mair has contended that the foundation of a state could be in
this development by a leader of a dependent and loyal body of
supporters. Slightly different is the individual among the Inuit who
is able to lord it over a community by his own physical force or use
of dreaded supernatural powers.

With the Big Man, anarchy can then degenerate into tyranny.
What sometimes occurs may be seen as an abortive attempt to
introduce a governmental-state system. It is invariably a failure
because there is a definite ambivalence within the community
towards authority, so that if established it regularly inspires
rebellion and the Big Man who tries to be the bully is most
often murdered. Thus, the situation returns to an acephalous or
more anarchic condition. In addition, there is no precedent for
establishing a succession pattern so as to perpetuate a dynasty. It
is also clear the New Guinean and other systems do not develop
permanent states out of their Big Man leadership pattern because
there is no adequate economic, technological or organisational
base. The New Guinea Big Man is limited by the productive

capability of his dependents and this is inhibited by lack of a more complex technology. Nor can one expect to control extensive territories with the available, very simple, methods of communication and transportation. At the same time the Big Man's power is maintained and extended only through a network of personal contacts. There is no organisation of loyal bureaucrats to sustain the realm. The difference between king and Big Man is fundamental: kings receive tribute and submission; Big Men must rely on support (Schneider, 207). "Rather than being a stage in the evolution of government, the state, or rather the monarchy, is but a point on one end of a spectrum whose other end is stateless societies containing only big men" (Schneider, 207).

Leaders among the Ifugao represent yet another type of Big Man. In their role as go-betweens they have the legitimate right to command contending parties to mediate, on threat of violence. Government then, in a most limited sense, has been instituted.

Clastres believes that the state cannot rise out of the 'chiefly' role, but this view requires some modification. First, it is least likely to arise in those cases which clearly fit the qualifications of centripetal leadership. Here it does not arise because the community is vigilant in restraining the chief. Nevertheless the Anuak village chief exemplifies a leader of this sort who, under certain circumstances can apparently expand his authority. Secondly, the sort of anarchic leadership characterised by the Pygmies is even less conducive to state development. Not only does the community frown upon any vigorous exercise of authority, but individuals have been conditioned to avoid the aggressive affirmation of leadership. Thirdly, the state as a permanent institution has difficulty in appearing in those centrifugal systems such as in New Guinea for reasons we have just enumerated. On the other hand, a governmental institution may be more likely to appear in connection with certain kinds of mediator roles as among the Ifugao. But, also significant in this regard are the roles of Holy Men. To be sure, Clastres sees these as different from his centripetal style chiefs and recognises the possible emergence of government in the role of prophet among the Guarani Indians in South America.

Hocart has argued that the earliest government-like functions were assumed by ritual specialists, some of whom, in the course of time, become fully fledged rulers of states as part of the general process of increasing specialisation in the division of labour. In Marxist theory power derives primarily, if not exclusively, from control of the means of production and distribution of wealth, that is, from economic factors. Yet, it is evident that power derived from knowledge — and usually 'religious' style knowledge — is often highly significant, at least in the social dynamics of small societies. The Australian leader derives his power by his control of esoteric ceremonial knowledge, the Inuit shaman by his control of curing techniques and the manipulation of the dark arts. The Nuer leopard skin chief has the power of the curse as do the elders and rainmakers among the Lugbara. The foundation and legitimacy of the Anuak chief's role is in its ritual and supernatural significance. Economic factors are hardly the only sources of power. Indeed, we see this in modern society as well, where the capitalist owner does not wield total power. Rather technicians and other specialists command it as well, not because of their economic wealth, but because of their knowledge. For the anarchic polities we have looked at it is clear that the functionaries with knowledge are often entitled to invoke sanctions which at least border on the legal. As was just noted above the Ifugao case as well as the Nuer and Lugbara suggest that the germs of government often first appear as the mediator role is transformed into a judiciary one, which also has ancillary police-like powers. A separate and distinct police force would presumably be a later development.

Countless authors agree that the state arises with social differentiation and increasing social complexity. Such views often implicitly argue that the state becomes a necessity as an integrative device. This is apparently the thesis of Wittfogel, who in his hydraulic theory of state origin correlates the rise of the state with the development of extensive irrigation systems. The latter necessitate co-ordination and the state is the grand co-ordinator. Much data has been assembled to demonstrate that complex social arrangements, whether irrigation works (eg, the Ifugao) or the international postal system, are co-ordinated in lieu of the state. In addition, of course, the fact that the state does appear constantly in connection with highly complex social arrangements does not mean that it *must* occur, nor that it *ought* to appear.

Oppenheimer among others argued that the state originates out of conquest. The expansion of one group so as to conquer another gives rise to an apparatus aimed at maintaining domination. The major drawback to a conquest theory of state origin is that before a group embarks on the war path it has already become a state. The examples Oppenheimer presents are of social entities which were states when they commenced expansion.

Anarchic polities engage in hostilities which are best not confused with warfare, but rather should be called feuding. This is because, among other things, true warfare entails the organisation of armies with a chain of command and with the intent of subjugating an enemy and occupying his territory. For those societies we have investigated above, it is apparent that some have the germs of governmental organisations, but they engage in neither real warfare nor in conquest. In other words, some kind of governmental structure is perhaps an essential prerequisite to engaging in the true warfare necessary for conquest. One requires at least the rudiments of an administrative system to order new subjects about. At the same time the truth of Oppenheimer's theory is that pursuit of warfare and conquest invigorates a burgeoning state and helps elaborate the administrative hierarchy. State and conquest are best seen as mutually interdependent phenomena which 'feed back' on each other.

Intrasocial conflict affords another explanation of state development. The Marxist theory of class conflict is the most notable of such theories. It argues that where there is an economically dominant class there is a state and where there is no state there is no class system. Marxist theory identifies property accumulation with the evolution of the state. And such a correlation was made as well by anarchists. Kropotkin and Bakunin both believed the abolition of capitalism — private property — was a prerequisite to the building of an anarchist society. Proudhon, however, saw that private property, which is used to intimidate, exploit and subdue others was in truth 'theft' and incompatible with anarchy, but individual property not so employed was not. Our survey of anarchic polities seems to substantiate Proudhon's view. The societies we have encountered recognise individual ownership of important resources and where, as in New Guinea, those resources are frequently used as devices to create a body of dependents we have 'Big Men' who take on a more tyrannical character than leaders in other anarchic polities who do not seek to acquire economic control over others.[1]

The Marxists Barry Hindiss and Paul Hirst have claimed that with "the primitive and advanced communist modes of production" there is no state because there are no social classes. Such a view ignores the bureaucratic-managerial elite as a class, thus unveiling one of the weaknesses of Marxist theory. That is, the bureaucrats as non-property holders are not seen as a social class and so are not seen as worthy of further consideration. Yet they are nevertheless a potent social force which perpetuates the division of society

---

[1] Modern anarchists face a dilemma if they propose the abolition and prohibition of private property, in that in order to do so they would seem to require an institution suspiciously like a state to ensure its abolition and to ensure that it remained abolished.

into the powerful and the powerless. Such observations are not intended as a demonstration of the falsity of a class theory of state origin. Rather they are intended to question the absoluteness and dogmatism with which this theory is sometimes enunciated. Neither government nor social class can be developed to any extent without the other also appearing. The case of ancient Iceland demonstrates that social classes can exist without the state, but not for long. Governmental functions restricted to the local headman as a kind of proto-state require no class or rulers, but a full blown state with government applied to extensive areas and large populations does. And those who control and own the society's wealth will certainly be part of the ruling class.

Often leaders in stateless societies have been transformed into governmental officials as a consequence of contact with already existing nation-states. It was noted above that people bordering on China's northern frontier no doubt created states as a consequence of the role of their notables as intermediaries, especially in the trading activity. Among Afghan tribes men of influence assume the role of chief liaison agent between their own people and a neighboring state. Increasingly they come to accumulate the trappings of governmental authority themselves and so help create states. Similarly, European colonial powers in the process of their territorial aggrandizement on contact with people in stateless societies recognized certain individuals as "chiefs" of the "tribe" and insured for them formalized power positions. Thus, stateless societies are either transformed into states themselves or are absorbed into existing states.

All the relevant case material presented here concerns societies which for the most part exhibit only rudimentary forms of government and social class. They suggest, then, that in what might be seen as the earliest phases of state development there are alternate paths of social change. Ronald Cohen has written: ". . . [T]here is no clear cut or simple set of causal statements that explains the phenomenon of state formation. . . The formation of states is a funnel-like progression of interactions in which a variety of pre-state systems responding to different determinants of change are forced by otherwise unresolvable conflicts to choose additional and more complex levels of political hierarchy." Once this is achieved there occurs a convergence of forms towards the early state (142). Yet clearly involved in the beginnings of state formation is an inter-dependent development of government and social class tied to an economy which is able to provide the means to sustain an elite class. Hierarchy, submission and tribute are characteristics of any fully-developed state and these cannot properly bloom until society has the proper wherewithal, economic and otherwise "to deliver the goods"

Even more fundamental ingredients for state formation are the individual will to power and the creation of a division between leaders and led. From these basic elements we have noted several different paths for further elaboration in the direction of the state. Thus leaders, in their capacity as mediators may acquire authority to impose legal sanctions, first possibly in a restricted sense and eventually broadening the realm of control. Other kinds of leaders may build a loyal body of dependents who in turn legitimise the use of force by the leader. In these cases wealth and knowledge are important bases for establishing one's credit as a ruler. Men's associations may assume governmental functions and if these are in the hands of age grades we might expect the system to be more democratic. In some instances we have encountered, such as New Guinea, the seed of statism has been planted, but has never truly germinated. In others, as the Tiv or the Ibo, there is only the most limited growth; there is an anomalous condition with the barest rudiments of the state. State development may be a subtle and insidious process by which the distinction between leader and led is transformed into one between ruler and ruled. In looking at anarchic polities one can only discern at best the very beginnings of this development — the prelude and first lines of the first act in the drama.

I suspect that one of the most common scenarios for state (and class) development commences in the initial anarchic polity with the existence of some kind of 'big man' who was at one and the same time a recognized mediator of disputes, an impressive manipulator of supernatural forces and above all a central figure in a redistribution system in which he held impressive feasts for and made loans to a considerable number of individuals who consequently became his dependents and retainers. As the big man thus enhanced his wealth and power, trade increases, labor specialization becomes more widespread and populations increase, particularly as a consequence of improved productivity. The social order then becomes more heterogeneous, composed of groups with increasingly divergent interests and outlooks so that intergroup conflict becomes more common and more important. Thus, the mediator and mystagogue roles of the 'big man' are augmented. He can turn some of his dependents and retainers into armed guards and enforcers abandoning his role as mediator for that of arbitrator-ruler. Thus, human societies which once were all egalitarian, acephalous and anarchic entities are transformed into hierarchic, authoritarian states. At the same time some of the more favoured henchmen of the 'big man', through their own machinations and especially through being able to establish themselves as centers of lesser redistribution systems are able to increase their own wealth and power so that they are increasingly differentiated from the rest of society. An elite class of controllers of wealth and power with the 'big man' at the top is created over a subordinate class of producers of wealth.

Finally, Pierre Clastres has made an interesting observation on the phenomenon of state formation, although he might slightly overstate the case. He maintains that the shift from hunting-gathering to Neolithic agriculture is not a decisive revolutionary change since old patterns of social organisation were not altered that radically. In addition the Middle American states were dependent upon an agricultural system of the same technical level as the anarchic 'savages' of the forest. The real revolution is the rise of the state and of 'hierarchical authority', not economic transformation. ". . . (P)erhaps one must acknowledge that the infrastructure is the political, and the superstructure is the economic" (171). Thus, is Marx turned on his head.

Does anarchy have a future or is history a one way street?

Whether anarchy has any future requires us first to consider how to dispense with the state which now prevails everywhere. Secondly, we may inquire into the general pattern of historic and cultural trends regarding state development and the prospects for a libertarian age from that vantage point.

Three general techniques for abolishing the state and government have been most commonly proposed by anarchists. One advocates undermining the state by the creation of a multitude of voluntary associations whose functioning will make the state superfluous. Another favours violent revolutionary overthrow. A third approach is non-violent direct action, which includes such a syndicalist technique as the labour strike. Why anarchists avoid electoral politics should be obvious from what has already been said about anarchism. But, in short, anarchists have no faith in such a technique because they do not believe one can defeat an enemy by joining him.

The attempt to make the state superfluous was popular amongst the early 19th century anarchists. Proudhon hoped to initiate at least the decline of the French state by a proliferation of mutual associations which would loan money interest free. Several Americans including Josiah Warren had similar ideas, particularly entailing monetary reform and mutualism, which were seen as paths to the free society. Much later, Gustav Landauer wrote: "The state is not something which can be destroyed by a revolution, but it is a condition, a certain relationship between human beings, a mode of behaviour. We destroy it by contracting other relationships, by behaving differently."

Another approach along these same lines is the intentional community. Indeed, Josiah Warren saw his communities as demonstration experiments which people would be able to observe, be impressed by and copy. Always the anarchic intentional community is an attempt to 'contract other relationships', to 'behave differently' and find alternatives to the state.

But many who seek to 'build the new within the shell of the old' are essentially indifferent to the ultimate fate of the state. For many who have participated in intentional communities the motivation is a personal one: of finding immediately a different, and presumably better, life for themselves and their families. They are unconcerned about its potential consequences upon the state, or at least that is of very secondary significance. Yet, some who are interested in building mutual associations in part as devices to undermine the state, simultaneously pronounce the obvious anarchist truth that the state is an institution which will not voluntarily abdicate its power. Those in power would never come to see themselves as superfluous and, as they have done on countless prior occasions, they will act to suppress any perceived threat to their positions. The state in a modern capitalist society, as in Canada and the United States, may readily tolerate, even encourage, credit unions and co-operatives and any number of other mutualist voluntary associations. This support would soon turn to suppression if such movements became a threat to the banking and corporate interests of the country. In addition, such organisations readily tend to become 'establishment' oriented. Rather than having a modifying effect upon their environment, it is the environment which modifies them in a more conservative direction. Co-operatives, for example, are notorious for becoming as large, as bureaucratic and nearly as capitalistic as the more traditional organisations. Do not misunderstand. I am all in favour of mutual associations and of Landauer's call to contract other relationships. However, such techniques are extremely limited and it is hard to see how, by themselves, they can produce a transformation to a stateless society because, by one means or another, no state will permit it to happen.

Another course of action suggested by anarchists is violent overthrow of the state. We have seen the use of violence as a diffuse sanction amongst various anarchic polities. Yet this seems inconsistent with an ideological commitment to the doctrines of anarchism. Violence is the technique of the state and the ultimate form of coercion. Those who adopt it as a means cannot help but be tainted by its use. A main reason for the anarchist rejection of participation in the governmental process is that it will have a corrupting effect upon individuals, turning them into politicians seeking power and personal glory. No less can be the case for those who take up violence in the attempt to find justice. Yet the strongest arguments against anarchist resort to violence is that any effective violence necessitates a military structure which must clearly be the most anti-anarchist form of organisation conceivable. Can one imagine an army organised on anarchist principles of voluntary co-operation and consensus? The implications and logical consequences of pacifism would seem to be anarchism. The view of some Quakers that there can be a non-violent state or government is self-contradictory since the state is by definition based upon violence. Otherwise it is not a state and must be a polity based on other than legal sanctions. Conversely anarchists who would be the first to recognise this inherent nature of the state, have often justified war and in this sense have sought to use statist methods to abolish the state.

Bakunin expected the revolutionary zeal of the masses to be spurred on by a group of selfless devotees who had no care for themselves or their own glory. They were to be a body of strong, educated personalities who would not seek to lead, master or direct the masses. Instead, they would learn what the people desired, articulate it and, with their broader knowledge and understanding, better be able to aid in pushing the revolution towards the goals set by the masses. This vanguard would be an anonymous and invisible body blended into the background. Thus, in part is the justification for Bakunin's romance with secret conspiratorial groups. The revolutionary vanguard Bakunin saw being drawn from the large number of 'declassed intellectuals' and middle class students, "children of peasants or the lower middle class, the children of unimportant civil servants and bankrupt gentry" — any who have no chance of pursuing a career or position (Lehning, 189). Lenin was influenced by this Bakuninist idea, but as a 'realist' his vanguard had lost all the high-minded altruism which Balkunin, in his romantic and naive way, held to be imperative. In contrast to the fascists, whose elite is a vanguard of heroes, Bakunin's is a vanguard of saints.

In general, any proposal to build the barricades is today a purely romantic notion which is strategically stupid. Military technology has become so sophisticated and expensive that only governments can invest in it and support it. A guerrilla army would find itself faced with overwhelming odds and its only hope would be to incite the military to join the revolution — a most unlikely event.

The third technique, that of non-violent direct action, is the viable alternative to violent revolution. It requires much self-discipline and patience, demanding that one be satisfied with miniscule successes and slow transformation. Certainly this, coupled with the movement to build voluntary, mutualist associations, is the only approach having much feasibility. Yet no prospects can be promising, particularly when one looks at the general trend of history.

The anarchic polities we have discussed in this essay are largely phenomena of the past. Anarchies have been transformed into subject entities by colonialist states and then gobbled up by third world nations. Their old social structure has been modified so as to accommodate to the proper functioning of the modern state. The lineage elder is now a 'chief', who may call upon the local constabulary for aid; the mediator becomes the judge who now commands. 'Indigenous' anarchies are a dying breed, an endangered species. This process seems to support the contention that the main thrust of history is towards the creation of states and authoritarian forms. It is a movement from decentralisation to centralisation, from small to big. While we may cite case after case of the growth of states out of an earlier anarchy and have noted the several germs of statism in our examples, the evidence of anarchy evolving out of the state is next to non-existent. Indeed, not only is the trend towards state organisation but it is towards bigger and fewer states enveloping the world.

Recently Robert Carniero showed how the number of polities (of all kinds) in the world has, since at least 1000 BC, continually declined. "And not only has there been a decrease in the number of autonomous political units in the world; the tendency has accelerated. It is quite clear that the rate of decrease in the number of independent political units between AD 500 and AD 1976 was much greater than it was between 1000 BC and AD 500" (Carniero, 214). Overall, during the 3,000 year period from 1000 BC to the present, he estimates the decline has been from several hundred thousand polities to 157 in 1976. We may cavil that the latter figure is too small since it includes only the world's nation-states and fails to take into account the fact that in many parts of the world there are cultural groups which persist as autonomous political entities despite the claim of some nation to the territory. Still the decline is dramatic and, what is more, it would be yet greater for anarchic polities since we must assume that a high proportion of societies in 1000 BC were of this type, while few if any are today.

Carniero attempts to project the approximate time we must anticipate the creation of a single world state. He arrives at, not

1984, but about 2300. Such projections can be discounted as rather fanciful, but what cannot be overlooked is the clear major trend towards fewer and bigger states.

The usual argument against anarchy runs something like this: people are not perfect; they require constraints; the bad need to be confined in jails. The moment one institutes a free society based on voluntary co-operation there will arise people who will seek to take advantage of the situation and accumulate power themselves. Further, as societies become larger and more dense in population and more heterogeneous, the problems of order and decision-making become too complex to be left to consensual techniques and diffuse sanctions. So from this vantage point as well there are pressures to centralise, institutionalise and formalise authority patterns.

Anarchist theoreticians have long warned of the dangers entailed in the assumption of power even by the most idealistic. Bakunin particularly attacked Marxism along these lines. He was rightly somewhat more than suspicious of the 'dictatorship of the proletariat' and correctly predicted that it could be "nothing else but despotic rule over the toiling masses by a new, numerically small aristocracy of genuine or sham scientists" (Maximoff, 287). Later W Machajski, a Polish participant in the Bolshevik Revolution, came to similar conclusions about the Soviet Union, for as he saw it the proletarian revolution had been transformed into a dictatorship of the party hacks. Arguments along these lines were further expanded by Max Nomad.

In 1911 Roberto Michels published his *Political Parties* in which he expounded the 'iron law of oligarchy'. This law states that all organisations develop in the direction of increasing authoritarianism, bureaucratic and oligarchic rule. Whoever says organisation says oligarchy. To demonstrate his thesis Michels analysed the history of the several European political parties. Later Seymour Lipset and others sought to refine Michels' interpretation by studying a labour union, the International Typographers Union, which did not seem to follow the pattern of the inevitable move towards oligarchic rule. From this investigation Lipset and his cohorts suggested some conditions which might preclude a bureaucratic and authoritarian development. Interestingly enough they entail little an anarchist theoretician might not have told him: small units, a variety of autonomous local voluntary associations, several interest groups none of which can control or monopolise power, no great differences in socio-economic status and a general state of economic security for all, an educated population and one which shows a high degree of participation in communal affairs, a high sense of group solidarity, and leaders who are not given much salary or status difference. In other words, 'chiefs' must be servants — impotent co-ordinators in a centripetal relationship. I would also suspect that a conscious will of the membership to preserve a free society is no small factor in this process.

Perhaps the Industrial Workers of the World is another example which deviates from Michels' law and for reasons similar to those Lipset found for the typographers. Yet while we may scout about looing for exceptions, the prevailing directions seem in accord with the 'iron law of oligarchy'. Thus, among labour unions, for the one or two which have avoided this direction there are 100 which have not.

Aside from the general trend for complex organisations to develop internal changes which produce oligarchy, there is yet another type of observable trend which commences with voluntary associations and ends as well in an authoritarian structure. This pattern was pointed out by Bert Buzan in a paper on 'Voluntary Co-operation and Social Democracy: The Case of 20th Century Neo-Populism' delivered at the International Symposium on Anarchism (1980). Buzan reviews the history of the farmer-populist movement in the United States between 1880 and 1920 and notes that it originated with various apolitical voluntary mutual aid associations. The most important of these were co-operatives aimed at marketing farm products. These, however, met with the concerted opposition of vested economic interests. Thus railroads refused to carry their goods; land and buildings were not available for sale or rent for grain elevators and warehouses. Because of this sabotaging by capitalist enterprises the members turned increasingly to electoral politics spawning the Peoples Party, Farmer-Labour Party and Non-Partisan League. In their devotion to seeking reform through government, they moved away from voluntary co-operation to depend more on formal legislation. At the same time, of course, the co-operative organisations themselves became large, bureaucratic and political lobbying groups (in line with Michels' predictions). Thus, in addition to an internal dynamic which pushes an organisation towards oligarchy, there is the external process which propels individuals to abandon those voluntary associations they have in favour of dependence upon bureaucratic and governmental ones.

Now the question arises, perhaps the movement towards centralised oligarchy is only part of a long term historical process of oscillation between decentralisation and centralisation. Yet it is difficult to find examples of trends towards decentralisation — at least of a libertarian nature. Periods of so-called cultural or organisational decay in history may suggest this sort of trend. But what trends do occur in these situations is the creation of a number of petty despotisms out of one which had existed before. Decentralisation is not accompanied by freedom. The revolutions and revolts of history and the decay of social systems have invariably entailed the replacement of one kind of despotism by another. Or what is a process of decay of one polity is the basis for the creation of another, so that, for example, the appearance of Clovis' Frankish kingdom and of the Umayyad caliphate follow on the heels of the decline of Rome. Power abhors a vacuum. A few South American Indian societies referred to above appear to have become anarchic as a consequence of a general process of tribal disintegration. Yet this situation seems uncommon and is limited to extremely tiny polities. Those few societies such as the Pygmies, which provide not the slightest hint of embarking upon the course towards a governmental or state organisation, are also small and highly homogeneous without any specialisation of task. They exemplify that rarity wherein members have been diligent in restraining the forces of authority and wherein events have been such that members have not been detracted from that noble pursuit. Perhaps one must conclude that the main thrust of history is towards centralised states with occasional minor 'pulsations' of reaction — slight and temporary reversals or people running off on alternate paths. Perhaps also the last decade and a half has experienced a feeble resurgence of this kind in parts of the Western world. Thus, there is not only the enormous increase in the number of communal experiments, but there is the movement of individuals 'back to the land', to simplification of life and revolt against the establishment. More important has been the appearance of mass social movements based upon 'segmented polycephalous idea-based networks'. Unfortunately these several activities remain largely confined to the offspring of middle-class white society alienated from the values of their parents.

Back in 1963 Paul Goodman in *People or Personnel* pointed out how centralisation has now made industry inefficient, creating excessive congestion and problems of transportation and communication. With the diffusion of electric power it is possible and more sensible to decentralise production. This theme has been reaffirmed continually. Schumacher harks back to Kropotkin and Goodman, noting how 'small is beautiful'. Recognition that small group operations and decentralisation can be more productive and obviously more humane, is coupled today with some growing recognition of the inefficiency and alienating effects of large impersonal, centralised organisations. Recently

Marshall McLuhan offered a mixed prediction for the 1980s. It was mixed in the sense that part foresees greater decentralisation by the expanded use of the home computer, TV, telephone and other 'electric software'. But it is not necessarily a prediction of individual liberation in that with this expansion of new technology McLuhan sees a further disappearance of personal identity — the disembodiment of individuals and a new form of government by 'pollstergeists'.

In spite of the various 'recognitions', hopes and predictions, and in spite of the movements into the intentional community or out to the land, states continue to become more powerful and centralisation goes on essentially unabated. Certain biological species are reputed to have become so specialised that they cannot adapt to changed environmental conditions and so become extinct. Perhaps there is a parallel to the potential fate of those social systems which become so utterly complex and overburdened with top down administration that they collapse. Hopefully, out of the remains might arise, like a Phoenix, a simplified and decentralised system. But would this only generate its own tyranny?

Humans as intelligent beings have some control over their own destiny. As they increase their knowledge and understanding in the world and, particularly, of their own behaviour, they should better be able to manipulate their environment and modify their social order so as to make life more agreeable. Yet knowledge and understanding are intimately tied up with values and priorities of values. They are circumscribed as well by the apparent fact that humans appear to be rather conservative beasts willing to change from the known to the unknown and the untried only in the direst emergency. Therefore, while presently there may be a greater realisation of the possibility of a '1984 world', other priorities than freedom and individuality may have precedence. Further, this possibility is not perceived as an immediate and overwhelming threat. When we consider the numbers who persist in such a simple thing as cigarette smoking, in spite of the overwhelming evidence of its relation to cancer, how can we expect people to be concerned about such more abstract and apparently less obvious matters as threats to personal freedom?

Not only is anarchy unlikely to be achieved because of the improbability of dispensing with the state, but even given the abolition of that institution, the prospect for subsequent modes of organisation remaining decentralised, autonomous and free is as doubtful as the likelihood of the participants being truly dedicated to 'freedom, equality and justice for all'.

I have already earlier in this book suggested the kind of free society which might be more durable and resistant to corruption. Namely, it would be one in which each person and group was involved in a complex web of mutual relations such that each bond within the web would act as a counter-balancing force to every other. In this way every participant would be constrained and unable to expand his or her realm at the expense of any other.

Proudhon saw human societies as being engaged in a struggle between 'freedom' (anarchy) and 'authority'. But he was imbued with the rather naive 19th century notion of progress and optimism. He had faith in the eventual victory of the forces of freedom. An Australian group — the Sydney Libertarians — has, one might say, adapted Proudhon to the latter part of the 20th century. They envisage a perpetual struggle between 'freedom' and 'authority'; neither one of which will be annihilated.

It appears, indeed, that we are left with a politics of perpetual protest. There cannot be any point at which those dedicated to liberty can sit back in security and assume the world is in peace, harmony and freedom. That a truly free society may never be attained or, if achieved, would have the most tenuous life is clearly no excuse to abandon the struggle. If we resign ourselves to what is, there would hardly be much point in living. And, even if anarchy were to be achieved, eternal vigilance would be the bare minimum price for even a modicum of success. Despite what the international anthem of the revolutionary class might say there is no final battle. The battle is forever.[1]

---

[1] Perhaps this might be called the anarcho-cynicalist point of view.

Bibliography

AVRICH, PAUL (ed), *The Anarchists in the Russian Revolution*, Cornell, 1973.

BARCLAY, HAROLD B, 'Segmental Acephalous Network Systems',*The Raven*, II, 3, 1989, also *Guru Nanak Journal of Sociology*, VIII,1,1987.

BARTON, RALPH, *Ifugao Law*, University of California Publications in American Archaeology and Ethnology, XV, 1919.

BERNDT, RONALD and P LAWRENCE (eds), *Politics in New Guinea*, University of Western Australia, Perth, 1971.

BICCHIERI, MG (ed), *Hunters and Gatherers Today*, Holt, Rinehart and Winston, 1972.

BIRKET-SMITH, KAJ, *The Eskimo*, Methuen, 1959.

DE LA BOETIE, ETIENNE, *The Politics of Obedience*, Black Rose Press, Montreal, 1975.

BOHANNAN, LAURA, 'Political Aspects of Tiv Social Organization' in Middleton, John and David Tait.

BOHANNAN, PAUL, *Social Anthropology*, Holt, Rinehart and Winston, 1963.

—'The Tiv of Nigeria' in Gibbs, James

— 'You Can't Do Nothing', *American Anthropologist*, LXXXII, 3, 1980.

BOURDIEU, PIERRE, *The Algerians*, Beacon, Boston, 1962.

BRENAN, GERALD, *The Spanish Labyrinth*, Cambridge, 1962.

BUBER, MARTIN, *Paths to Utopia*, Beacon, Boston, 1958.

CANNON, WALTER, 'Voodoo Death', *American Anthropologist*, XLIV, 1942.

CARNIERO, ROBERT L, 'Political Expansion as an Expression of the Principle of Competitive Exclusion' in Cohen and Service.

CLARKE, MV, *The Medieval City State*, Methuen, 1926.

CLASTRES, PIERRE, *Society Against the State*, Urizen, New York, 1977.

COHEN, JOSEPH J, *In Quest of Heaven*, Sunrise History Publ. Comm., New York, 1957.

COHEN, RONALD, 'State Foundations: A Controlled Comparison' in Cohen and Service.

COHEN, RONALD and ELMAN SERVICE (eds), *Origins of the State*, Institute for the Study of Human Issues, Philadelphia, 1978.

COLSON, ELIZABETH, *The Plateau Tonga of Northern Rhodesia: Social and Religious Studies*, Manchester University Press, 1962.

— *Tradition and Contract: The Problem of Order*, Aldine, Chicago, 1974.

CONDOMINAS, GEORGE, 'The Primitive Life of Vietnam's Mountain People', in *Man's Many Ways*, Richard A Gould (ed), Harper and Row, 1973.

CULSHAW, WJ, *Tribal Heritage*, Lutterworth Press, London, 1949.

DAHRENDORF, RALF, *Class and Class Conflict in Industrial Society*, Stanford, 1959.

DAMAS, DAVID, 'The Copper Eskimos', in Bicchieri, MG.

DENTAN, ROBERT, *The Semai: A Nonviolent People of Malaya*, Holt Rinehart and Winston, 1962.

DOLE, GERTRUDE, 'Anarchy Without Chaos: Alternatives to Political Authority Among the Kirikuru' in Swartz, Turner and Tuden.

DOLGOFF, SAM (ed), *The Anarchist Collectives*, Free Life Editions, New York, 1977.

DRIVER, HAROLD, *Indians of North America*, Chicago, 1962.

DRUCKER, PHILIP, *Northern and Central Nootkan Tribes*, Bulletin of Bureau of American Ethnology, Washington, 1951.

— *Cultures of the North Pacific Coast*, Chandler, San Francisco, 1965.

DURRENBERGER, E.PAUL, 'Stratification without a state: the collapse of the Icelandic Commonwealth', *Ethnos*, LIII, 3-4, 1988.

DYSON-HUDSON, NEVILLE, *Karamojong Politics*, Oxford, 1966.

ELKIN, AP, *The Australian Aborigines*, Angus & Robertson, Sydney, 1961.

ENGELS, FREDERICK, *The Origin of the Family, Private Property and the State*, Pathfinder, New York, 1972.

EVANS-PRITCHARD, EE, *The Political System of the Anuak of the Anglo-Egyptian Sudan*, London School of Economics, Monographs in Anthropology, 1940s.

— *The Nuer*, Oxford, 1940b.

— *Nuer Religion*, Oxford, 1956.

— 'The Nuer of the Southern Sudan' in Fortes and Evans-Pritchard.

FIRTH, RAYMOND, *Essays on Social Anthropology and Values*, Athlone, London, 1964.

FORTES, MEYER, and EE EVANS-PRITCHARD, *African Political Systems*, Oxford, 1961.

FRIED, MORTON, *The Evolution of Political Society*, Random House, 1967.

FRIEDMANN, ROBERT, *Hutterite Studies*, Mennonite Historical Soc., Goshen, Ind. 1961.

FROMM, ERICH, *Man for Himself*, Rinehart, 1947.

GEDDES, WR, *Nine Dayak Night*, Oxford, 1961.

GELLNER, ERNEST, *Saints of the Atlas*, Weidenfeld & Nicolson, 1969.

GIBBS, JAMES (ed), *Peoples of Africa*, Holt, Rinehart and Winston, 1965.

GJERSET, KNUT, *History of Iceland*, Macmillan, 1925.

GLUCKMAN, MAX, *Politics, Law and Ritual in Tribal Society*, Aldine, 1965.

GOODMAN, PAUL, *Drawing the Line*, Random House, 1946.

— *People or Personnel*, Random House, 1964.

GOODY, JACK, *Technology, Tradition and the State in Africa*, Oxford, 1971.

GREEN, MM, *Ibo Village Affairs*, Praeger, 1964.

GULLIVER, PH, *The Family Herds: A Study of Two Pastoral Tribes in East Africa: The Jie and Turkana*, Routledge and Kegan Paul, 1955.

—'The Jie of Uganda' in Gibbs, James.

HALLOWELL, A IRVING, *Culture and Experience*, Univ. of Pennsylvania, 1955.

HAMMOND, PETER B (ed), *Cultural and Social Anthropology*, Macmillan, 1964.

HARDY, DENNIS, *Alternative Communities in Nineteenth Century England*, Longmans, 1979.

HART, DAVID, 'Clan, Lineage, Local Community and the Feud in a Riffian Tribe', in Sweet, Louise (ed), *Peoples and Cultures of the Middle East*, Natural History Press, 1970.

–'Rejoinder to Henry Munson Jr.' *American Anthropologist*, XCI, 3, 1989.

HINDES, BARRY and PAUL HIRST, *Pre-Capitalist Modes of Production*, Routledge and Kegan Paul, 1975.

HINE, VIRGINIA, 'The Basic Paradigm of a Future Socio-Culture System', *World Issues*, II 1977, pp.19-22.

HOBSBAWM, ERIC J, *Primitive Rebels*, Manchester University Press, 1959.

HOCART, AM, *Kings and Councillors*, Chicago, 1970.

HOEBEL, E ADAMSON, *The Law of Primitive Man*, Harvard, 1961.
— *Man in the Primitive World*, McGraw-Hill, 1958.
HOGBIN, IAN (ed), *Anthropology of New Guinea*, Melburne University Press, 1973.
— *The Leaders and the Led: Social Control in Wogeo, New Guinea*, Melburne University Press, 1979.
HOLMBERG, ALAN, *Nomads of the Longbow*, Smithsonian Institution, Washington, 1950.
HONIGMANN, JOHN J, *Ethnography of the Fort Nelson Slave*, Yale, 1946.
— *Culture and Ethos of the Kaska*, Yale, 1949.
HOSTETLER, JOHN A, *Amish Society*, Johns Hopkins, 1963.
— *Hutterite Society*, Johns Hopkins, 1974.
HOWELL, P.P., *A Manual of Nuer Law*, Oxford, 1954.
HUGHES, DIANE, 'Kinsmen and Neighbors in Medieval Genoa' in Harry A Miskimin, David Herlihy and AL Udovitch, *The Medieval City*, Yale, 1977.
JENNESS, DIAMOND, *The Carrier Indians of the Bulkley River: Their Social and Religious Life*, Bulletin of the Bureau of American Ethnology, 1943.
KLIMA, GEORGE, *The Barabaig: East African Cattle Herders*, Holt, Rinehart and Winston, 1970.
KROEBER, ALFRED L, *Handbook of the Indians of California*, California Book Co, 1953.
— *Configurations of Culture Growth*, Univ. of California, 1944.
KROPOTKIN, PETER, *Mutual Aid: A Factor in Evolution*, Heinemann, London, 1902.
— *The State: Its Historic Role*, Freedom Press, London, 1943.
LANDAUER, GUSTAV, *For Socialism*, Telos, St Louis, 1978.
LANGNESS, LL, 'Traditional Political Organization' in Hogbin, Ian, 1973.
— 'Bena Bena' in Berndt and Lawrence.
LEE, RICHARD B, *The Kung San: Men, Women and Work in a Foraging Society*, Cambridge University Press, 1979.
LEHNING, ARTHUR (ed.), *Michael Bakunin: Selected Writings*, Grove Press, New York, 1973.
LEVAL, GASTON, *Collectives in the Spanish Revolution*, Freedom Press, London, 1975.
LEVI-STRAUSS, CLAUDE, *Tristes Tropiques*, Atheneum, New York, 1964.
LEWARNE, CHARLES PIERCE, *Utopias on Puget Sound 1885-1915*, University of Washington, 1975.
LIENHARDT, GODFREY, 'The Western Dinka' in Middleton and Tait.

LIPSET, SEYMOUR, MARTIN TROW and JAMES COLEMAN, *Union Democracy*, Doubleday, 1956.

LODGE, EC, 'The Communal Movement in France' in CAMBRIDGE MEDIEVAL HISTORY, Vol V, 1926.

LOWIE, ROBERT, *The Origin of the State*, Rinehart, 1927.

—'Social and Political Life of the Tropical Forest and Marginal Tribes' in Steward, Julian (ed), *Handbook of South American Indians*, Vol V, 1949.

—*Social Organization*, Holt Rinehart and Winston, 1960.

MAINE, HENRY, *Ancient Law*, Murray, London, 1861.

MAIR, LUCY, *Primitive Government*, Penguin, 1962.

MACHAJSKI, WACLAW, 'On the Expropriation of the Capitalists' in Calverton, VF (ed), *The Making of Society*, Random House, 1937.

MALINOWSKI, B, *Crime and Custom in Savage Society*, Kegan, Paul, Trench and Trubner, London, 1932.

MARSHALL, LORNA, 'The Kung Bushman of the Kalahari Desert' in Gibbs, James.

MARTIN, JAMES J, *Men Against the State*, Libertarian Book Club, New York, 1957.

MARTINES, LAURO, *Power and Imagination*, Alfred A Knopf, New York, 1979.

MAXIMOFF, GP, *The Political Philosophy of Bakunin: Scientific Anarchism*, Free Press, Glencoe, Illinois, 1953.

MICHELS, ROBERT, *First Lectures in Political Sociology*, Harper, 1949.

—*Political Parties*, Dover, 1959.

MIDDLETON, JOHN, 'The Political System of the Lugbara of the Nile-Congo Divide' in Middleton and Tait.

—*The Lugbara of Uganda*, Holt, Rinehart and Winston, 1965.

MIDDLETON, JOHN and DAVID TAIT, *Tribes without Rulers*, Routledge and Kegan Paul, London, 1958.

MUKHERJEA, CHARULAL, *The Santals*, Mukherjee Co, Calcutta, 1962.

MUNSON, HENRY JR., 'On the Irrelevance of the Segmentary Lineage Model in the Moroccan Rif'; *American Anthropologist*, XCI, 2, 1989.

MURDOCK, GEORGE P, 'The Common Denominator of Cultures', in Linton, R, *The Science of Man in the World Crisis*, Columbia Univ, 1945.

NADEL, SF, *Black Byzantium*, Oxford, 1942.

NOMAD, MAX, *Aspects of Revolt*, Noonday Press, 1959.

—*Masters: Old and New*, Black Cat Press, Edmonton, Alberta, 1979.

ORANS, MARTIN, *The Santal*, Wayne State University Press, 1965.

ORENSTEIN, HENRY, 'Asymmetrical Reciprocity: A Contribution to the Theory of Political Legitimacy', *Current Anthropology*, XXI, 1980.

PARETO, VILFREDO, *Sociological Writings*, Praeger, 1966.

PEHRSON, ROBERT N, 'The Lappish Herding Leader: A Structural Analysis', *American Anthropologist*, LVI, 1954.

PELLICANI, LUCIANO, *Red Bureaucracy*, Black Cat Press, Edmonton, Alberta, 1979.

PIRENNE, HENRI, *Early democracies in the Low Countries*, Harper and Row, New York, 1963.

POSPISIL, LEOPOLD, *The Kapauku Papuans*, Holt, Rinehart and Winston, 1963.

PREVITE-ORTON, CW, 'The Italian Cities Till c 1200' in *Cambridge Mediaeval History*, V, 1926.

PROUDHON, PIERRE J, *The General Idea of the Revolution in the Nineteenth Century*, Freedom Press, London, 1923.

—*The Principle of Federation*, Toronto, 1979.

—*What is Property?*, William Reeves, London, No date.

RADCLIFFE-BROWN, AR, *The Andaman Islanders*, Free Press, Glencoe, Ill, 1948.

—*Structure and Function in Primitive Society*, Free Press, Glencoe, Illinois, 1952.

READ, KENNETH, 'Leadership and Consensus in a New Guinea Society', *American Anthropologist*, LXI, 1959.

RICHARDS, VERNON, *Lessons of the Spanish Revolution*, Freedom Press, London, 1953.

RITTER, ALLEN, *Anarchism: A Theoretical Analysis*, Cambridge Univ, 1980.

ROCKER, RUDOLF, *Nationalism and Culture*, Rocker Publications Comm, Los Angeles, 1937.

RÖRIG, FRITZ, *The Medieval Town*, Batsford, London, 1967.

SAHLINS, MARSHALL, 'Poor Man, Rich Man, Big-Man, Chief: Political Types in Melanesia and Polynesia', *Comparative Studies in Society and History*, Vol V, 1963.

—*Tribesmen*, Prentice-Hall, 1968.

SCHNEIDER, HAROLD K, *Livestock and Equality in East Africa*, Indiana University Press, Bloomington, Indiana, 1979.

SCHUMACHER, ERNST, *Small is Beautiful*, Harper and Row, 1973.

SCHURTZ, HEINRICH, *Alterklassen und Männerbünde*, Reimer, Berlin, 1902.

SERVICE, ELMAN, *Primitive Social Organization*, Random House, 1962.

—*The Hunters*, Prentice-Hall, 1966.

—*Origins of the State and Civilization*, WW Norton, 1975.

SHARP, LAURISTON, 'People without Politics: The Yir Yiront' in Hammond, Peter.

SOMERS, GEORGE E, *The Dynamics of Santal Traditions in a Peasant Society*, Abhenav Publs, New Delhi, 1977.

SPENCER, ARTHUR, *The Lapps*, Crane, Russick and Co, 1978.

SPENCER, B and GILLEN, F.J., *The Arunta*, Macmillan, London, 1927.

SPENCER, ROBERT F, *The North Alaskan Eskimos: A Study in Ecology and Society*, Bulletin of Bureau of American Ethnology, Washington, 1959.

SPOONER, LYSANDER, *Let's Abolish Government*, Arno Press, New York, 1972.

STEWARD, JULIAN, *Basin-Plateau Aboriginal Socio-Political Groups*, Bulletin Bureau of American Ethnology, Washington, 1938.

STEWARD, JULIAN and LOUIS FARON, *Native Peoples of South America*, McGraw-Hill, 1959.

SWARTZ, MARK, VICTOR TURNER and ARTHUR TUDEN (eds), *Political Anthropology*, Aldine, 1966.

TAIT, DAVID, 'The Territorial Pattern and Lineage System of Konkomba' in Middleton and Tait.

—'The Political System of Konkomba' in Ottenberg, Simon and Phoebe (eds), *Cultures and Societies of Africa*, Random House, 1960.

TAYLOR, MICHAEL, *Anarchy and Cooperation*, John Wiley, 1976.

THOMAS, ELIZABETH M, *The Harmless People*, Random House, 1958.

THOMPSON, LAURA, *The Secret of Culture*, Random House, 1969.

TREITSCHKE, H VON, *Politics*, Harcourt, Brace & World, 1963.

TURNBULL, COLIN, *The Forest People*, Doubleday, 1962.

—'The Mbuti Pygmies of the Congo' in Gibbs, James.

TURNER, VICTOR, *The Ritual Process*, Aldine, 1969.

TYLOR, EDWARD B, *Anthropology*, Watts, London, 1946.

UCHENDU, VICTOR, *The Igbo of Southeast Nigeria*, Holt, Rinehart and Winston, 1965.

VEYSEY, LAURENCE, *The Communal Experience: Anarchist and Mystical Communities in Twentieth-Century America*, Chicago, 1978.

VINOGRADOV, AMAL, *The Ait Ndhir of Morocco: A Study of the Social Transformation of a Berber Tribe*, University of Michigan, 1974.

VOLINE, *The Unknown Revolution*, Libertarian Book Club, New York, 1955.

VORREN, O and E MANKER, *Lapp Life and Custom*, Oxford, 1962.

WARNER, W LLOYD, *A Black Civilization*, Harper, 1958.

WATANABE, HITOSHI, 'The Ainu' in Bicchieri.

WATSON, JAMES B, (ed), *New Guinea: The Central Highlands*, Special publication of *American Anthropologist*, 1964.

—'Tairora' in Berndt and Lawrence.

WEBER, MAX, *The Theory of Social and Economic Organization*, Free Press, New York, 1964.

WINTER, EDWARD, 'The Aboriginal Political Structure of Bwamba' in Middleton and Tait.

WISSLER, CLARK, *Man and Culture*, Crowell, New York, 1923.

WITTFOGEL, KARL A, *Oriental Despotism*, Yale, 1963.

Index